MORE AND BETTER PHEASANT HUNTING

"Driven Pheasants"

Original etching by David Hagerbaumer (Courtesy of Collectors
Choice, Santa Ana, California)

MORE AND BETTER PHEASANT HUNTING

Steve Smith

Winchester Press
An Imprint of New Century Publishers, Inc.

Printing Code
11 12 13 14 15 16

Library of Congress Cataloging-in-Publication Data

Smith, Steve.
    More and Better Pheasant Hunting.

    1. Pheasant shooting.   I. Title.
SK325.P5S68   1986   799.2'48617   86-19100
ISBN 0-8329-0417-1

DEDICATION

For Dad, who shot the first rooster I ever saw on the longest shot I ever saw, and then let me carry it home.

ACKNOWLEDGMENTS

I'd like to say thanks to some people for helping with this book. To photographers and friends Joe Workosky, Jerry Warrington, Tom Carney, and Bryan Bilinski for helping me with photos, and to Chuck Lichon for the foreword.

To Dave Meisner, Jim Wooley, Dave Duffey, and Gene Hill for answering some questions and giving you, the reader, more insight into the world of pheasant hunting.

To Bob Elman at Winchester Press, who made sure I was always painfully aware of deadlines, and to the various game departments whose contributions are appreciated.

To my kids, who during the time I spent writing this book (rather than helping them with their homework) managed to raise their grades.

And finally, to Sue, who knows how hamhanded I am and stepped in and typed the manuscript. You helped, all of you, and I'm sure none of you will let me forget it.

Steve Smith

vi

CONTENTS

FOREWORD

Around about the time Steve Smith was delivered into this world, the pheasant populaton in his native Michigan was nothing short of incredible. Human expansion and "advanced practices" relative to farming and chemical use had yet to catch up with the areas these magnificent birds had occupied.

Unfortunately for Smitty, and the rest of Michigan's pheasant hunters, the decrease in the pheasant numbers in Michigan was inversely proportional to the growth stages of this recognized outdooor author. About the time he was old enough (not to be confused with "capable enough") to handle a single-shot 20, pheasants started their downswing and eventually hit an all-time low around the late 1960s.

But this never prevented Smith from becoming addicted to the sight of his setter assuming a stylish point on a mature ringneck, or the sound of a cackling rooster bursting out of a weed-choked fencerow. These experiences, once instilled in a youngster's gray matter, are never forgotten. And the yearning to once again meet the challenge of these fine gamebirds will always surface during the traditional October 20 Michigan opener.

Steve's desire to continue seeking the challenge led him to travel the Plain States whenever time and finances allowed, and sometimes when they didn't.

All this "work" (as he so glibly indicates on his tax forms) has allowed him to become somewhat of an authority on keeping his tax payments below those of a felonious monk, as well as developing the necessary credentials for writing a book on the greatest gamebird of all.

A few short years ago I invited Steve and his older son Chris on a pheasant hunt in Michigan's Thumb region, one of the last strongholds for Michigan's dwindling pheasant populaton. I felt, as I know Steve did, that Chris's presence echoed days gone by when the two of us worked stubble fields and cut corn rows with our own dads in search of the ringneck. It was as if time had reversed itself 25 years.

I had hunted this particular square mile on the opener a week earlier, and had enjoyed what I considered a surprisingly good hunt. We knew the remaining birds would be "holed up" in the thicker brush, and consequently we would have to work especially hard for them. At one point, I sent Steve along with my Labrador retriever Jill into a tanglewood and thornapple thicket in an attempt to push out a bird or two—Smith is always a pushover for going into areas that would rebuff a rattlesnake. (He was always the one wearing the Orvis brush busters, so he was elected.) My intuition was right. Jill flushed a nice rooster at the end of the heavy growth, but we didn't get a shot. Eventually, it glided into a field of waist-high grass 400 yards away. I blew twice on the whistle, and Smith obediently worked his way toward the sound; Jill followed.

We converged on the place where the ringneck had settled down, Steve and I flanking Chris. The boy needed no coaching—he intently watched with gun in the ready position, waiting patiently for Jill to once again pick up bird scent.

Even though we knew the bird was within hearing distance of the click of the safety on our guns, the anticipation of the explosive flush of the bird was enough to send our blood pressure soaring.

But Chris, having been well coached on grouse and woodcock, was up to the test and dropped the bird at 30 yards with his first shot. As we stood admiring his wild Michigan rooster, Steve and I didn't say a word—the ear-to-ear grin on Chris's face said it all.

These are the kinds of stories that Steve has thoughtfully placed between the covers of this book—along with advice for novice and veteran alike.

Technically qualified, a journalist in the most professional sense, storyteller extraordinaire, analyst, witty humorist, and even, during one or two weak moments, a truth-teller—that's Steve Smith.

Chuck Lichon
Wildfowl Magazine

PREFACE:
A Brief Historical Perspective on the Ringneck

Under the auspices of the Smithsonian Institution, the great ornithologist Arthur Cleveland Bent published 22 thick volumes (originally and with bureaucratically inspired modesty designated *Bulletins*) on the life histories of North American birds. Among these impressive monographs was a tome of nearly 500 pages on gallinaceous birds, first published in 1932—by which time the pheasant was gratefully regarded as a very American bird.

"The cock ring-necked pheasant is a magnificent bird," wrote Bent, "and the display of his brilliant plumage and beautiful form to the best advantage before the demurely plumaged hens may well arouse their admiration and passion. . . . When suddenly startled, pheasants flush with a loud metallic whir of the wings, but not so thunderous as that of the ruffed grouse. Occasionally a bird flies off almost silently. They are able to shoot up nearly vertically if they are hemmed in by trees or a building, and they make off at a great speed. . . . The alarm notes, emitted when the birds are startled, are most commonly heard. These are loud and hoarse croakings . . . suggestive at times of an old domestic hen."

Suggestive, perhaps—indeed, quite similar—but Mr. Bent surely would have agreed that no sound in nature is quite like the raucous cackle of a flushed rooster: at once angry, alarmed, defiant, strident, as flamboyant as his plumage and as beautiful to a hunter.

Of the origins and Americanization of the pheasant, Bent noted that the bird "is generally believed to be of Asiatic origin and at a very early date *Phasianus colchicus* was introduced into Europe," but he added that some ornithological historians believed at least one subspecies (the so-called English pheasant) to have been indigenous to Europe. The European variety lacked the white collar of the bird we call the ringneck until the Chinese, or ringnecked, pheasant was introduced into Europe and the British Isles. By the late 19th century, "nearly all English pheasants . . . had some trace at least of a white collar." In connection with the bird's American heritage, Bent pointed out that "although some of the earlier English settlers in North America called the ruffed grouse the pheasant, a name that is still retained in the southern part of its range, no true pheasants are native, nor were they successfully introduced into America until 1881, when Judge O. N. Denny, then American consul general at Shanghai, China, after a previous unsuccessful attempt, sent 30 ring-necked pheasants to Oregon."

Of course, pheasant hunting—that is, the sport of wingshooting rather than the earlier practice of netting the birds over "setting" dogs—was popular in Europe as early as the 18th century. In America, pheasants were imported and stocked by such eminent wingshooters as George Washington, Governor James Montgomery of New York, and Ben Franklin's son-in-law, Richard Bache. All efforts to establish the birds in the wild or breed them over a long term were unsuccessful, however, until Judge Owen Denny shipped those Chinese pheasants to his brother's farm near Corvallis, Oregon. Of those 30 birds, 26 survived and were released in the Willamette Valley, where they thrived and proliferated.

Two years after the initial importation, another batch was shipped to Oregon—a kind of breeding reinforcement that may or may not have been needed by the original contingent, which was begetting and multiplying at a rate recalling the "begats" of the Old Testament. Within a decade, the birds had spread through the entire Willamette Valley. These ringnecks were commonly called Chinese pheasants but, as Bent noted, they were also known as Denny pheasants in recognition of the man who brought them to our land. That name was a fine gesture, and one that some of us would like to continue. We thank you, Judge Denny.

Five years after the Judge introduced the ringneck to the West, the first successful introduction on the East Coast was made by Rutherford Stuyvesant, who brought over a number of birds from England and released them on his estate in Allamuchy, New Jersey. During the following decade, still more were shipped from England to Massachusetts and then to other states. By the early years of the 20th century, they were established in at least 10 states and spreading fast.

They were not always appreciated by hunters nor loved by farmers. Being large, strong, and aggressive, pheasants were sometimes charged with driving quail out. Actually, what diminished the bobwhite coveys was the accelerating change in agricultural methods—the loss of habitat that would later harm the pheasants, too. Ringneck competition caused no harm to native birds. Some introductions of "exotic" wildlife have certainly caused havoc and decimation among native species, but the pheasant was a rare bird in the sense that it took up residence in an unoccupied or sparsely occupied ecological niche. Hence its success. Hence its harmlessness to other birds. (In some regions, in fact, it may have served to increase other avian populations by providing a new source of food for predators—acting as a "buffer" to lighten predatory pressure on native prey species.)

At one time, there was a great deal more justification for the antipathy of farmers. Certainly they liked a pheasant on the table as well as anyone, but there were decades when the farmers had fallen on hard times and the pheasants hadn't—yet. "The economic status of the bird," Bent noted, "whether harmful or beneficial, is dependent on local conditions and seasons of the year, and on the proportion between weed seeds and injurious insects eaten on the one hand and cultivated crops on the other. Pheasants are at times very destructive to sprouting corn and even to corn in the ear." No one would argue with the statement that they like corn—and grain of all sorts—not to mention garden crops such as beans and peas, with occasional snacks of beets, tomatoes, and assorted other delicacies. Yet today's farmer, on the average, is eager to set aside some acreage once devoted to corn and plant it for pheasant cover. The modern change in agricultural methods (and economics) has resulted in an ironic turn-around.

In the Midwest and in large parts of the East and West, farming practices benefited pheasants until the 1940s, when the birds reached peak populations. But the ringneck, like man, does not live by corn alone. The bird needs its larder speckled and streaked with hedges, fencerows, windbreaks, groves, brush, swamp, potholes—meaning sufficient water and a great deal of cover. As diversified family farms gave way to single-crop corporate agribusiness in the '50s, pheasants dwindled. Government policies sometimes made the situation worse by encouraging farmers to retire a lot of acreage, leaving it fallow in a totally unproductive way: plowed and bare. Although the Soil Bank program helped a great deal in some areas, federal policies tended to fluctuate—and so did wildlife populations.

Those populations (not of every species but of many, including pheasants) are now rising again, and the outlook with regard to governmental encouragement is very promising. So is the rising population of pheasants.

Economy has a great deal to do with this. The ringneck brings hunters and hunters' dollars, a factor that has not escaped the notice of the Department of the Interior and the Department of Agriculture, and one that has had a lot of attention from state fish and game departments. There have been experimental stockings of (and interbreedings with) Manchurian, Japanese green, and Caucasian blackneck pheasants for the sake of hardiness, reproductive potential, flushing and flying characteristics, and even resistance to Midwestern winters without benefit of sufficient windbreaks. There is no shortage of potential stock, since *Phasianus colchicus* has scores of geographically scattered subspecies, ranging from the Caucasus to China and Formosa.

Some regions have been much more successful than others in establishing self-renewing pheasant populations. Back in the 1920s, the great naturalist and game manager Aldo Leopold, often called the Father of Modern Conservation, first advanced the theory that calcium requirements limit the natural range. A laying hen pheasant needs more calcium than birds evolved on this continent, and pheasants will therefore thrive only as far south as the Ice Age glaciers carried heavy lime deposits—or in unglaciated pockets of habitat that are rich in lime. Since Leopold's time, it has been found that additional factors include the right amount of moisture, as well as ground temperatures that don't soar too high during the hatching season (plus the aforementioned food and cover). The experiments continue. And let us all be thankful that some of the experiments promise to bear fruit in the form of fowl.

I
THE BIRD

Most of us who hunt gamebirds today got our first taste of wingshooting on pheasants. We may have dallied with quail, got sidetracked on woodcock, or become enamored with grouse, but we'd probably want to spend our last day and our last shell on a rooster pheasant cackling at us like we're dirt.

The morning mist lifts enough to reveal a short, 12-year-old boy clutching a $15 20-gauge double shotgun. Only the right barrel is loaded. He shivers in the morning cold. In front of him a few feet, soggy cornstalks fade into the fog. Out there somewhere are the drivers, men and their dogs walking the field, hoping to push rooster pheasants ahead of them and into the air for the boy. The boy has already achieved coffee-shop immortality by missing 14 consecutive shots at pheasants; he is determined not to miss.

Out of the corner of his eye, he catches a movement on the ground. A proud rooster pheasant struts across the corn rows. Wet feathers detract not at all from his bearing. The boy tries to figure the best way to make the bird fly. He knows that if the bird keeps walking, it will soon be near the drivers and will probably double back; the boy's dad has told him that's what they do. With 14 misses on his record, the boy lifts the 20, sights down the barrels, and lightning-strikes the bird on the ground.

As he races for his prize, the morning mists close in around him and swirl into a time warp, dropping him a quarter-century later in an Iowa milo field. A rooster pheasant is hurtling ahead of a spanking west wind—35 yards out, 25 yards up, its tail snaking behind. He is standing behind another boy, a European-built double broken over his arm.

"Lead him, Son," the boy-now-man croons to the freckle-faced kid. "Keep swinging." The youngster's 20 double—only the right barrel loaded—streaks ahead of the bird. The freckle-faced kid's shoulder lurches; the wind and adrenaline steal the 20's crack. The bird flinches, its wing-beats become labored, and 35 yards out and 25 yards up, it dies.

The boy-now-man claps his son's back. "Nice shot, Chris! And remember, always take them in the air."

The pheasant in the boy's gamebag is just as satisfying a load as another one in the morning mists 25 years before. But things have changed in 25 years—and may now be changing again.

As most of us know, the first really successful establishment of pheasants occurred in the 1880s in Oregon. Transplanting and additional imports helped the bird take root wherever soil conditions contained the right amount of lime for eggshells and moisture to help in incubation.

Before a species is imported, biologists have to determine if there is a niche, presently unoccupied, which could be filled by the new species. In the case of ringneck pheasants, the niche apparently was totally empty, because the birds multiplied so fast that 11 years after their 1881 importation, a season was held in which 50,000 birds were shot.

Since that time, the bird has changed, not because it has produced generations of runners, although I'm sure pheasants are getting smarter and may run more often than fly, but because it has had to adapt to changing social and agricultural conditions.

As a species, pheasants are pretty lucky when it comes to being plagued by parasites and disease—they really don't have much of a problem. As we'll see later, the real problems come about through the fatal interplay of declining habitat and the effects of weather.

Although this isn't a natural history book, I think you should know something of the bird's habits—aside from the fact that they run like pro basketball guards. Pheasants live on a variety of foods—over 500 different kinds have been documented—but the majority are of the group we'll call grains: soybeans, corn, sorghum heads, milo, and so forth. As gallinaceous birds, pheasants store food in a crop which looks like a plastic bag suspended where the neck passes through the large breast muscles. Later on, the food moves down through a gizzard, where it is ground up with the aid of grit or gravel. A crop is really a survival tool for prey birds—birds which are often eaten by predators. A crop allows a pheasant (or quail or grouse) to scoot out, jam down a cropful of goodies, and scurry back into cover, thus exposing himself to predators for only a short time. Best for the bird's survival, then, is habitat that has good protective cover near a source of food.

Pheasants court, copulate, and nest in the spring. Hens are most successful in rearing chicks in areas with a high content of calcium in the soil—limestone. That's why the pheasant's range is limited to areas where this mineral exists, provided the weather is temperate.

A hen will lay about a dozen eggs, and she's on her own after mating; the polygamous male has moved to some other sweet young thing. Many roosters—especially those with long tails—accumulate harems of hens, mating with each in turn as she's ready; he's *always* ready.

The usual successful rooster/hen ratio is one rooster to three or four hens, not the 1:30 you often see quoted. One old boy who is now in the Rooster's Hall of Fame may have handled 30 ladies, but in the wild, 1:4 is pretty good.

Nest losses and egg losses result from a variety of causes, not the least of which is man. Roadside mowing destroys nests and hens, which squat at the proper level on their nests so that the mowing machine has little trouble lopping off their heads. Likewise, the first cutting of alfalfa—that's hay to you city boys—comes when pheasants are nesting. Alfalfa is great nesting cover—dense, hard for predators to move through, and often holding abundant insect life that the chicks will need later. So, Mama Pheasant heads for the hayfield when the nesting urge hits her. Trouble is, the hay cutting also takes place then, and few farmers ever notice a flopping, decapitated hen and a smashed nest.

Hard rains, hailstorms, unseasonably hot and cold spells, raccoons, skunks, snakes, coyotes, feral cats, farm dogs, foxes, crows, owls, hawks—the list of predators is long. They take the eggs, the chicks, or Mama Pheasant—whatever they can get claw and tooth into, but predators are natural problems and can't be compared with losses brought about by mowing.

Some states are enacting legislation to stop roadside mowing, or at least are delaying it well into summer until the nesting female has done what it is she has to do. It's a great idea—so great that I wonder what ever possessed politicians to vote for it.

Losses are bad among young birds through predation and weather, but also through run-ins with cars and farm machinery. What makes it worse is that a hen whose nest is destroyed will usually renest—but a hen that loses a brood is done. Her body chemistry has changed, and the remating and renesting urge has passed her by.

Young pheasants grow quickly. Like all ground nesters, the chicks are "precocial" and turn from balls of down to sprinting juveniles almost as you watch. Insects are important to young pheasants because bugs mean meat, meat means protein, and protein means bone and muscle tissue. All those unpronouncable chemicals dumped on fields to kill

A young bird in its first season normally has a lower mandible that will not support its body weight; lower beak will bend when grasped and bounced lightly.

The spurs of a young bird are rounded and gray in color . . .

off bugs don't do young birds a bit of good. The chicks weaken without the insect life, and are either more susceptible to predation or die outright.

But if things go well, they can fly in eight weeks, and at 21 weeks are colored up like the adults. Sometimes the birds we shoot in the early part of the autumn season are barely colored as roosters. Obviously, these birds are the results of late hatches brought off by a renesting hen.

The best way to age a rooster pheasant is by looking at the spurs; an old bird will have long, shiny, black ones that will cut you if you push on them too hard. A young bird's spurs are usually gray in color, rounded, and dull. Also, the

while those of a mature bird are longer, much sharper, and black. In any year, young birds make up the lion's share of hunters' bags. In the wild, the life expectancy of a pheasant is normally less than a year; the very high turnover is due to weather, habitat loss, and predation.

lower mandible (bill) of a mature bird will support its weight when you grab the bill and bounce the bird; a young bird's bill will bend and may even break. Like most gamebirds, the majority of pheasants bagged each season are young birds.

There seems to be a mistaken notion floating around that pheasants, depending upon where you find them, are different from one another—that they are somehow wilder in the East than in the Great Plains or in the West.

I don't happen to subscribe to that thinking. Instead, I think it's a numbers game. When we were all kids hunting with our dads, we could whistle up a farm mutt and head out to the back fields. We'd amble around, maybe stop-and-go a little, and we'd jump roosters. We'd shoot some—maybe even our limit—and head for the barn and chores. Today, throughout much of the bird's eastern range, that's not the case. We have to hunt hard and long to get a bird into the air. Talented and highly trained bird dogs are turned into quivering jelly by running roosters, and we curse the pseudo-evolutionary process which has created a race of runners.

This thinking process says that we have long ago shot those pheasants that would fly, leaving only those that like to leg it to pass their disgusting genes on to the coming generations, which will leg it even more as future hunting seasons fine-tune the population into runners.

Let's take a look at the bird throughout the year, not just during the hunting season.

Pheasants are preyed upon—depending upon their location—by the aforementioned foxes, coyotes, hawks, owls, housecats, dogs, skunks, weasels, raccoons, and probably a few other beasties I haven't mentioned. Most of them are landlocked—they can't fly. In the case of hawks and owls, these birds of prey much prefer a sitting, stationary target to one that is in flight. With all of its predators, the pheasant's best defense is flight. When a critter approaches, they take wing. Indeed, the highest predation on living birds takes place just after the chicks are hatched, before they are capable of flight. A pheasant that can't—or won't—fly is a meal for a fox or raccoon that will just chase until it catches up.

So, flight is the ultimate defense against most of the predators the pheasant faces each day of its life. Now, along comes pheasant season, and many of those that fly *are* shot; no argument here. But the bird is able to discern that this new threat—humans—is best eluded on foot. The human's dog is a different matter. Flushing dogs are so effective on pheasants because they simulate the hunting activities of the bird's normal predators. At the last moment before the pheasant perceives he's going to get caught, he jumps and flies, and we say that the dog "pushed it into the air." Not so, really—the bird just waited until he couldn't do anything else.

Now, back to the numbers game. If you've followed my thread of thinking this far, you've probably deduced that what we're talking about is that there are simply more birds in the Midwest and West. Habitat or genetics or whatever have conspired to produce higher populations there.

Let's say that 10 percent of all birds in a population will readily fly at the first hint of danger. I have no way of knowing if this percentage is accurate—I'm sure it isn't; it's just a number I'm using because my arithmetic isn't what it should be.

Now, let's further assume that on a Michigan or Pennsylvania farm there are 10 rooster pheasants—let's disregard the lighter hens, for whom flying is less of a chore and who have more to fear, because of nesting, from ground-bound predators and thus fly more readily than cocks do.

This means that on our eastern farm there is going to be one rooster that will jump within range when hunters approach. The hunter shoots it, then spends the rest of the day watching his dog cut didoes in the grass trying to catch up with the nine runners. He can't get close enough to do them harm, but neither could a fox, which is why they've survived in the first place. So the shooter heads for the barn to clean his bird, shaking his head about the damn running birds.

Let's stick our hero in a car and take him to Iowa and turn him loose on a farm out there. The farm is bigger, probably, and the pheasant populations are higher. The birds, less heavily hunted, are not as wary of hunters, true, but their main attribute is simply that there are more of them. Let's say that the same 10 percent ratio holds true, only the Iowa farm holds 50 roosters. Our boy puts five in the air, shoots his limit of three, and is happier than a clam. See? It's a numbers game.

The ringneck pheasant in this country is in trouble, compared to his glory years of the '40s through the early '60s. The most common explanation for the drop in populations is the clean-farming practices by agribusinesses which have allowed few places for the birds to live. But even in areas where suitable habitat exists, birds not only are lower in numbers, but it doesn't seem to take much to kill them off. Some biologists are starting to think the problem lies "not in our stars, but in ourselves"; that the birds we're dealing with are likely genetically inferior to those that made bird hunters out of our fathers.

The pheasant today is actually a combination of several strains of birds, and these strains may have passed on genes which, in their total, could create a bird not suitable for today's limited-cover conditions. Michigan has imported Sichuan pheasants (and eggs), a very hardy, smaller strain of bird which lives in China in some of the earth's most intensively farmed and populated areas. I've seen pictures of these areas, and you'd swear that an undersized hamster couldn't live there, but the Sichuan pheasants do. It's hoped that these birds and their ringneck hybrids can survive the harsh climate of the northern U.S. and can thrive in the smaller bits of cover which mark agriculture in the 1980s. If so, they will eventually augment the ringneck and fill the niche in the habitat that is marginal for both ringnecks and ruffed grouse.

Part of the reason for all of these changes is sociological and has to do with land-use practices. In the 1930s, at least in the East, pheasants were just coming on in good numbers. Farming methods were primitive compared with today's, and the Depression turned a lot of family farms into deeds gathering dust in a banker's vault. Then came the war—the farm boys marched off to fight, and farms went into production. The food was raised with basically old-time methods, but many acres were put into production. Crops and pheasants flourished—the wide fencerows making for good, year-round cover for the birds, and the "dirty" cropfields, relatively free of herbicides, providing food and cover.

I can remember my father telling me of the huge numbers of Michigan ringnecks he found on the family farm when he was home on furlough during the war, and the stories sound unbelievable. After the war, many of the boys did not go back to the farm. Instead, they took wives, produced Baby-Boom kids, and worked in factories in the cities, and we quickly became an urbanized nation. Still, the pheasant thrived because of the basically archaic farming methods.

But the rising human population made food production even more imperative, and technology gave us big tractors, combines the size of houses, pesticides, and herbicides. The urban sprawl drove up farmland prices, and more and more farm kids headed for the bright lights when they came of age, leaving less land and fewer people to raise more food. This was when the pinch on pheasants started.

Clean farming is simply working every available inch of land as intensively as possible. Sloughs were drained and planted to crops; ditchrows were tiled, covered over, and planted; woodlots were cut down and planted; fall plowing came in to save time in the spring; the big machinery was in use all the time because it simply didn't make any money sitting around.

Now there was obviously less cover, and the chemicals introduced into the food chain in the form of weed and bug killers had an effect as well. Where once a cornfield with its weedy rows could provide food and cover, it now provided only food. Fall plowing eliminated much of the critical wintering-over cover pheasants require. Weeds were killed in areas where they encroached into cropfields, thus depriving the birds of more cover.

And the pesticides, especially the now-banned DDT—illegal, but still in the food chain—weakened eggshells and caused unsuccessful hatching. The pesticides killed so many bugs that many pheasant chicks, which need insects for bone and muscle development, did not reach maturity.

Some predators, once shot unmercifully, are now fully protected, at least the hawks and owls. I'm not saying this is bad, but I *am* saying that often the avian birds of prey can have a staggering effect on pheasants, depending on the cover. With proper cover, the pheasants will escape; without it, they're sitting ducks. Some observers have recently suggested that perhaps there should be some form of predator control for the protection of pheasants. Hawks, for example, eat small rodents and larger mammals which prey on young pheasants and raise hob with pheasant nests. But these same hawks also eat pheasants. On shooting preserves and on English estates, with their high bird populations, hawks and owls are drawn to the fields like iron filings to a magnet. Hawks aren't all bad, we know; what some are suggesting is that perhaps they aren't all good, either, and maybe we should re-examine the predator's role.

Unfortunately, where predator control as it applies to pheasants *has* been looked at, notably in South Dakota and Minnesota, a couple of things came out. First, extensive predator control *did* raise the pheasant population—for that year; but losses to weather negated these gains. Secondly, the predator-control measures, to be effective, had to be almost total—thereby wiping out a lot of creatures. Thirdly, the expense was staggering—many millions of dollars would be required to make even a small, temporary dent in the predator population. Last, after only one year, the predators rebounded and things were about where they had started.

In a way, this is good because it shows that pheasants, given proper food supply and cover—good habitat, in other words—need no other help to avoid predators. It's up to us to provide that habitat.

When the public wants to "help" (and offers advice on things like predator control), things can get messed up a bit. I'm quoting now from the Minnesota DNR's Wildlife Section manual on pheasants:

"Stocking Pheasants—For many years, public clamor for initiating stocking, predator control, and winter feeding programs has been a thorn in the side of wildlife managers. Although these programs have been relatively popular with the public, they tend to divert the DNR's limited budget and manpower away from efforts to provide pheasants with balanced habitat.

"The general public often points to artificial stocking as a way to put more birds in the bag. Over the years, DNR wildlife managers have extensively researched the practice of stocking pen-raised pheasants. Let's review the three

State-reared, pen-raised pheasants, waiting for their tails to grow. This batch is destined to be breeders; therefore they are separated from the hens until spring.

types of stocking programs and the problems inherent in each.

"*Introductory stocking* is trying to establish a new species where good habitat exists. The introduction of the ringneck in Minnesota some 80 years ago is a remarkable success story. Stocking worked at that time because the newly introduced birds found a super-abundance of habitat and they did not have to compete with an existing population of wild birds. But times have changed. Pheasants now live in virtually every piece of suitable habitat. Attempts to introduce pheasants into habitats like the coniferous forests of northeastern Minnesota or the peat bogs of the north-central counties would be pure folly.

"*Maintenance stocking* is attempting to maintain or enhance an existing pheasant population by stocking additional birds. In the past, DNR biologists have trapped wild pheasants, then raised their offspring for releasing in areas

State pheasants being stocked. Stocking of any of the various types—put and take, maintenance, and introductory—is usually a waste of money, as is predator control. The single biggest factor determining the success of pheasant populations is habitat. If you have it, you'll have birds; if you don't, you won't. (MI DNR photo)

where severe weather had nearly decimated the wild birds. But these efforts were costly and did not produce good results.

"Stocking pen-raised birds is an even bigger waste of time and money. Each piece of habitat has a carrying capacity, or a maximum number of pheasants that it can support. The carrying capacity varies from season to season and year to year, largely depending on the quality of the habitat. Dumping additional birds into areas that have already reached their carrying capacity is futile, unless the habitat base—including nesting and wintering cover—can be expanded.

"The shock of being placed in a totally new environment and having to find food and cover is apparently too much for most pen-raised pheasants. Game-farm birds also lack an inborn wariness and are vulnerable to predators. A South Dakota study found that less than 7% of the roosters released in summer were harvested in fall. Only 4.8% of the released birds survived through winter. Another study in Wisconsin revealed that even if stocked hens make it through the winter, they produce almost no chicks (.4 to .8 young per hen) the following spring. In simple terms, if wild pheasants are having trouble surviving in what little habitat remains, game-farm birds would have even less chance.

"*Put-and-take stocking* involves releasing pheasants just prior to the season opener or just before a weekend. Its purpose is simply to provide extra shooting for hunters. New Jersey is among several eastern states that provide limited put-and-take shooting. Since 1965, that state has raised and released an average of 65,000 pheasants each year, at an annual cost of nearly $700,000. Game officials stock the birds only in state wildlife-management areas, which often become overcrowded with hunters. To ease the congestion, New Jersey has established controlled hunts on some areas. Hunters must register and wear arm bands as identification, so game officers can control hunter density.

"Minnesota wildlife managers are in the business of producing birds in the wild; they would rather leave put-and-take shooting to private enterprise. The state currently issues about two dozen licenses to private shooting preserves that offer that type of hunting."

Here's another one for you: Recently, some of the fellows at Penn State University released the results of a two-year study in which, using radio collars, they tracked pheasants which had been trapped in the wild and then re-released, another group which had been commercially reared, and still a third group which had been pen reared by the state's Game Commission.

After 100 days, they counted noses. Seems that 70% of the wild birds were still alive, 40% of the commercially reared birds were still around, but only 10% of the game-farm, pen-reared birds were alive. The report noted that most of the pen-reared birds were killed within two weeks by predators—mostly foxes but also hawks and dogs.

The state, as a result, is modifying its pheasant-rearing facilities to make things more wild for the birds prior to their release in the hope that the stocking program will produce a better bird for hunters.

Now, there's no surprise here—the wild birds have a better chance, and anything a government agency touches only comes out about 10% effective anyhow. But what *is* surprising is how quickly predators, notably the fox, can descend upon a group of birds which are not adequately strengthened for flight. Soon after their release, these birds could probably make only short flights and so in all likelihood would mostly run from foxes. (Remember the "generation of runners are more adaptable" theory I talked about earlier? Here's proof that running only gets you eaten. If you think for a second that pheasants are evolving into runners and not flyers because hunters are killing off the flyers, forget it. Running only gets a pheasant very dead, bird season notwithstanding.)

We've got a set of problems with pheasants in this country, problems that must be dealt with if the bird is going to continue to be a viable resource for recreational hunting into the next century.

There have been attempts in almost every state to put pheasants before hunters artificially—the "put-and-take" stocking concept. In some states, such as the New Jersey example, pheasants are pen-raised and then released into designated areas in hunting situations. These situations are usually artificial at best, disgusting at worst—birds that can't (not won't) fly, hordes of hunters, any semblance of

hunting manners and ethics forgotten—the list of trans-
gressions is long.

Not the least of the problems is the expense. A state-
raised bird is expensive—about two or three times what a
commercial operator can rear one for to sell to a shooting
preserve. And the preserve pheasant is a hardier bird.

One way around the cost of pen rearing is a program
that has been set up in several of the states where pheasants are having problems and some stocking, as the man
said, "couldn't hurt." Under this cooperative program, in-
volving such groups as the 4-H Club, Future Farmers of
America, and sportsmen's clubs, day-old pheasant chicks,
incubated and hatched under the auspices of the state, are
made available to the cooperators. The chicks are reared at
the clubs' facilities and released on land which the state has
determined ahead of time is good pheasant habitat.

There are a few drawbacks to this program, though,
which states have sought to combat. For example, in Michigan the birds have to be released no later than two weeks
before the opening of the general small-game season—the
pheasant season, in other words. This prevents groups from
just opening the pen doors on opening morning and having
a field day with birds the state gave them for free.

Another drawback is that if you haven't tried it before,
rearing and raising a bunch of baby pheasants into a bunch
of young adult pheasants isn't as easy as it sounds. The
recipients of the pheasants are required to attend an all-day
workshop on pheasant husbandry in which they are taught
things about behavior, feeding, care, space requirements,
projected losses, spotting diseases, combating predators, and
so forth. I'm not sure you can learn all of that in one day,
but the states are pretty good about answering any questions as they come up.

For those who are considering planting birds on land
which should hold pheasants but presently does not, there
are a few things to take into consideration. First, there probably won't be much carryover into the spring of birds re-

leased into the wild the previous fall. Food is in good supply then, but predator populations are at a peak in fall, and the losses to this source are very high.

Secondly, pen-raised birds released into the wild usually don't stray too far. Studies in Britain, where pheasants are artificially released until Katie has to go over and bar the door, show that over 60% of the birds do not stray more than 400 yards from the point at which they were set free, and less than 1% of the birds travel more than 1½ miles. This means, obviously, that you can't haul a cartful of pheasants out into a field, open the crates, and think the birds are going to naturally disperse over the entire region. If you want the birds evenly dispersed, you'll have to do it at the time of release.

And this dispersal is essential because the birds, congregated thus, are going to cause a congregation of predators and a depletion of the food supply, both factors conspiring to decimate the population of released birds.

Also from Britain come the results of a study paid for by The Game Conservancy. In that country, where 85% of the birds taken before the gun are pheasants, little is known of the behavior of natural, wild pheasants, especially as compared to the store of knowledge about pen-reared birds. The study notes that released birds which survive the shooting season must then contend with the predator situation.

Predators respond to an artificially high population of a prey species in two ways. First, the individual predator is likely to spend more time hunting in the area where he had his last hunting success—same as you—and secondly, this success usually leads to his success as a raiser of other predators. A fox, certain of a good food supply from abundant pheasants, will more than likely have more kits in a litter, all of which will then establish hunting areas and home ranges that correspond with the high population area of the pheasants. So the pheasant has to contend with more predators spending more time hunting. Not good if you're a pheasant. Couple that with a released bird's tendency to stay put rather than wander to new habitat, and it is obvious that released pheasants become sitting ducks.

Those birds—both released and wild—that make it through to the spring then go through the breeding and courtship displays. The cockbird displays a "harem defense" posture, not unlike that of a bull elk or buck whitetail. He gathers a flock of willing hens, breeds with them, and establishes his own breeding territory from which subdominant cocks ("satellites") are driven off. Once bred, the hens then establish feeding and nesting ranges within the male's larger breeding range, and the male watches over the troops. In his state of breeding fury, he may even take on small mammalian predators that are a threat to the nesting hens, and he certainly kicks the daylights out of any intruding, lesser males.

The hens have a tendency to choose for mating the rooster that displays most ostentatiously, has the most aggression, and seems to be the best protector. Some scientists think this choice is made by the hens based upon the length of a male's tailfeathers. Well, I've seen marriages between humans based on less, so why not?

In any event, the number of released birds that go on to become nesting natives is quite small, but some do, and if programs like the chick-rearing one I've described can help at all, great!

Land-use practices have always upset pheasant populations, for either the good or the bad. I outlined earlier how the growth in human populations and the clean-farming ethic affected pheasants from the 1930s to 1950s. Well, the boys in Washington didn't help, either.

For about 15 years, the Soil Bank program encouraged farmers to take acres out of production in order to hold down the harvest of grain, which the government had to buy through price supports. The Soil Bank days of the '60s were halcyon ones for pheasant hunters. Cover abounded, and the stories drifting east were amazing—South Dakota and Nebraska were Valhallas for pheasant hunters. Over 28 million acres were in the Conservation Reserve portion of the Soil Bank program.

Then, in 1970, this program was cancelled. Those acres were put back into production more intensively than they ever had been because of the sophistication of modern agricultural methods.

At about the same time, federal and some state programs were instituted which gave farmers the funds they needed to drain and plant wetlands on their property—such sloughs are prime cover for ringnecks. Then farmers were given money to straighten out streams and brooks that ran across their land and to cut down the attending brush, all in the name of better water control. Naturally, this vegetation was often pheasant cover.

Ever larger machinery came into play. Its use made small fields more difficult to plant and maintain, so what fencerows there were got taken down and the cover plowed under so that the $100,000 stereo/CB/tapedeck/air conditioning-equipped tractor could have a smooth shot at a mile of unencumbered field.

On top of all of this, in the 1980s, we have the small farmers going out of business and their farms being scooped up by huge agribusiness outfits. The small farmer was usually less tidy; being less productive—which may be why he went under—meant that his land may have held birds. But with his land foreclosed on and then bought up, the fencerows and tractors came in and the pheasants went away.

If this sounds like an indictment of farmers, it's not. If I were paying $5,000-$7,000 an acre for good land, I'd farm hell out of it, too; the farmer can't be blamed—it's what he does to make a living, and by doing so, he feeds us and a bunch of the world besides.

In the early winter of 1985, as I was compiling this book, things took a decided turn for the better for pheasants and pheasant hunters. It was then that Congress passed—and President Reagan signed—the 1985 Farm Bill. This bill is aimed at helping American farmers through one of their blackest periods, but many of the people who helped design

The way things look right now, this boy is going to be spending a lot of time bagging rooster pheasants. The Conservation Reserve section of the Farm Bill, passed in 1985, permits a total of 45 million acres to be taken out of rowcrop production, much of it potential wildlife habitat.

this bill and write it into law saw it as an opportunity to do something about the problems of soil erosion and dwindling wildlife habitat. Early reports have mentioned that some farmers aren't too thrilled with what they have to do to get and keep government aid in the form of price supports, loan guarantees, etc., but that only shows that the lunch is not free.

Part of the bill calls for acreage to be set aside in a Conservation Reserve—read habitat creation if you're the hopeful. The set-asides are both long-term (up to 15 years) and huge—a total of 45 million acres, including 5 million the first year, are proposed in the bill, which is now in effect. However, the actual acreage involved will be considerably less. Farmers place bids to have their land included in the Conservation Reserve, the overall purpose of which is to reduce soil erosion by taking marginal, erodible lands out of rowcrop production. The bids must be approved by the feds before the lands are actually enrolled in the Reserve. Farmers receive a variety of economic incentives for having their land in the program.

Jim Wooley, a field representative with Pheasants Forever—a group I'll tell you more about later—told me that the Farm Bill's Conservation Reserve section would approximate the Conservation Reserve portion of the old Soil Bank program. In 1960 there were 28 million acres doing pheasants some good; soon there may be millions more acres doing pheasants some good. Does this tell you anything? It should tell you that the Glory Years may be on their way back, and that a new generation of hunters may be able to experience unforgettable pheasant hunting. Let's hope.

Time will tell. I hate to get too optimistic, and Wooley told me that it will be a few years before acreage set aside under the new program grows up enough to become pheasant nesting cover, and still longer before it can offer adequate winter cover. Still, the potential is there, and it's a huge potential!

Pheasants Forever is a nonprofit wildlife conservation organization with over 14,000 members. Its function is to educate the public to the need for adequate habitat for wildlife—particularly pheasants. In this way, the organization is similar to Ducks Unlimited, the Ruffed Grouse Society, the Wild Turkey Federation, Trout Unlimited, and other single-species conservation groups.

Based in Minnesota, the group is raising funds for the purpose of education. Later it may acquire land, but it seems to me that the Conservation Reserve will provide the

The pheasant's future depends upon permanent habitat—cover that is there all year, providing birds with the critical wintering-over protection. This shooter took advantage of the wide strips of cover separating crop-fields. In looking for cover, smart hunters note the trees, large shrubs, and other signs of long-lasting permanence. Such areas act as magnets for pheasants as autumn progresses and cold, ice, and crop harvest deplete other, more transient cover. (photo by Joe Workosky)

land—PF can get involved in the education of the farmer. Pheasants Forever's address is: P.O. Box 75473, St. Paul, MN 55175. The group puts out for the membership a nifty little magazine that's devoted to the pheasant hunter—dogs, guns, conservation stories, and so forth. The publication alone is worth the basic $15 (tax-deductible) membership fee.

Now, all of us who are old enough to remember when all TV was black and white and when you could understand the lyrics to the No. 1 song, remember the Glory Years of pheasant hunting. Habitat that grew up in the Soil Bank days provided pheasants with what they needed.

Habitat is most important during the winter, the time of "the great leveling." I'm quoting the following from *The Pheasant in Minnesota*, published by the Minnesota DNR:

"Winter brings a day-to-day test of survival for ring-necks. Across the prairie farmland, the birds must persevere against weighty odds: subzero temperatures combined with winds up to 70 miles per hour, and storms that dump 15 inches of snow. To make matters worse, pheasants must still elude predators in cover that by now has become sparse and scattered.

"The December pheasant, however, is well equipped to survive the harsh winter environment. Its large size and strong muscles enable it to move freely over all but deep, fluffy snow. Healthy and strong, the bird is in peak physical condition. Its plumage is thicker than at any other time of the year, and layers of fat insulate its body while providing a source of energy.

"Despite its ruggedness, the ringneck lacks certain survival traits common to other gamebirds in the northland. Ruffed grouse and Hungarian partridge will burrow-roost in soft snow, which insulates them from the intense cold. But the pheasant, unless covered by a sudden, heavy snowfall, prefers to roost on the snow or in trees, where more energy must be expended to keep warm. And unlike bobwhite quail and partridge, pheasants will not huddle together to share body heat.

"To conserve energy, pheasants roost in heavy cover where the thick overhead tangle traps the air. Stands of giant ragweed or tall marsh vegetation like cattails, bulrushes, and wild cane provide good roosting, loafing, and escape cover. Many birds roost on frozen wetlands, snuggling into the thickest cattail stands they can find.

"When wetlands, drainage ditches, and roadsides fill up with snow, the adaptable ringneck heads for woody cover. Clumps of willows, alders, or other types of brush afford excellent cover. Many birds move into woodlots and shelterbelts where they roost in evergreen trees, usually six to 10 feet off the ground.

"Unfortunately, not all woodlots and windbreaks provide adequate winter cover. To provide adequate protection from blizzards, a shelterbelt must be at least 150 feet wide, contain an understory of low branches, and have one or more rows of dense shrubs around the north and/or west sides. Windbreaks with four or more rows of conifers on the south and east sides are best. The dense boughs break the wind and catch snow, while providing good overhead protection from winged predators.

"Pheasant feeding activity is more intensive and concentrated into shorter periods during cold weather, provided food is readily available. The birds start feeding before sunrise and by midmorning have usually settled into dense loafing cover. The most intense feeding period begins in late afternoon and continues until sunset.

"In most cases, pheasant roosting sites are within one-fourth mile of feeding areas. The birds seldom move farther than one-half mile from cover to food. Pheasants that must venture far to find food become vulnerable to severe storms, predation, and accidents. Roadkills, for example, often increase when birds are forced to search for food along snow-cleared highways.

"Foxes, owls, dogs, cats, and other predators are often hard-pressed to catch adult pheasants in summer. But they may find easy pickings when the birds move into the open or when they crowd into light cover.

A victim of clean farming, pesticides, and fall plowing, the ringneck pheasant has somehow adapted, although not in the numbers most hunters would like. How hardy is today's pheasant? Some biologists say that all the crossbreeding of various imported strains has manufactured a bird with less "toughness." Others point to "hybrid vigor" and commend the bird for doing as well as it has. Still, in areas where suitable habitat is present, pheasants are capable of populations reminiscent of the Soil Bank "Glory Days." (Joe Workosky photo)

"Ringnecks are tough, resourceful characters. During winter they frequent windblown fields where waste grain has been exposed. Where pheasants know the location of a pile of waste grain, they may scratch through 20 inches of compacted snow to get at the food. They also feed on weed seeds, fleshy fruits, and different parts of wild plants when the snow gets deep.

"The adaptable birds often congregate around corn cribs and grain bins, move into farmyards to feed among livestock, or pick waste grain from manure spread over a field. In South Dakota, about 85% of the pheasants in one study area lived in and around cattle feedlots during a particularly severe winter.

"With good cover and a source of food within one-fourth mile, pheasants can resist extremely cold temperatures. At 10° below zero, a healthy pheasant in thick cover can go without food for up to two weeks. Although they weigh less, hens can go without food as long as the roosters.

"Food shortages are most common in intensively farmed areas, where fall plowing has turned the landscape into a vast sea of black soil. Shut off from their major source of food, the birds begin dying when they drop to about 50 to 60% of their normal weight. During periods of extreme cold, starving pheasants will die at even higher body weights.

"A starving pheasant is unable to walk or fly normally, and usually dies in its roost. Its breast muscles will be shrunken so that its breast bone, or keel, becomes very prominent. It will have little or no body fat, an empty crop and gizzard, and a dark green or black gizzard lining compared to the normal light green. Starving birds may eat straw, parts of cornstalks, manure, and even carrion.

"Pheasant survival is usually best during winters with little snowfall. They suffer most during winters with a combination of heavy snows, strong winds, and lengthy periods of extreme cold. Sleet storms can also make the pheasant's life difficult by encasing its foods in ice.

"The worst possible condition for pheasants is a strong weather system that begins with sleet followed by blizzard conditions, and finally, several days of frigid temperatures. A St. Patrick's Day blizzard in 1965 wiped out over half of the (Minnesota) pheasant population in two days. The storm dropped 19 inches of snow, which in some areas piled up into drifts 14 feet high. And in the blizzard's wake came several days of subzero cold. Another devastating winter storm in 1975 eliminated from 50 to 65% of the birds in some areas.

"Severe winter storms kill in two ways. Most birds die from being buried within the deep drifts. Pheasants huddled in cattail marshes, brushy wetlands, and other cover that would be perfectly adequate during a normal winter may be quickly entombed by the drifting snow. In some cases, however, pheasants that become entombed are better off than birds on the surface. If the snow is not too deep, the birds can often force their way out.

"Caught in the open or in light cover, a pheasant may die from exposure. The deadly combination of searing winds and subzero temperatures may cause ice and snow to build up between the bird's feathers. The plumage no longer insulates the bird. It starts to lose body heat and soon dies. Many birds tolerate the bone-chilling winds just so long, then abandon their hiding spots, apparently to find better protection elsewhere. But once they leave cover, they succumb quickly.

"The savage storms of winters past demonstrate the sad plight of Minnesota's pheasant population. Without good cover, many birds will continue to perish in severe winter storms. But with an abundance of good-quality habitat, pheasants can survive the worst nature can dish out and quickly replenish their losses."

Habitat and weather, then, go hand in hand. In mild winters marginal habitat will give pheasants enough cover from wind, cold, snow, and predators to allow them to survive nicely. In harsh winters, the habitat—the cover—must be much thicker and more extensive.

For example, in Iowa the winters of 1980 and 1981 were quite mild. In northern Iowa, where habitat for pheas-

A recent Chinese import, the Sichuan pheasant is capable of living in very marginal cover, but it lacks the white ring and overall size of the familiar ringneck. It's hoped that this bird, when crossbred with ringnecks, will inhabit the cover types that are fitting for neither pheasants nor ruffed grouse. The Sichuan's habits of feeding on buds and roosting in trees will help during deep-snow winters, according to Michigan wildlife biologists. Purebred Sichuans will be released to see how they adapt to the northern pheasant range. (MI DNR photo)

ants is marginal at best, the birds survived nicely, and there were bumper crops of pheasants. Then came the winter of 1981-82. The weather was horrible. Folks froze to death in stalled cars on the Interstates. I was living in Iowa at the time, and a stretch of five straight weekends found me literally snowed inside the house. The pheasant population dropped, especially in the areas of marginal habitat, which just wasn't good enough to support the birds under those conditions.

Good habitat will support a large number of birds under the worst potential conditions. Brother, that means a *lot* of good habitat. That's why so many people are pleased with the 1985 Farm Bill—it should provide just that kind of habitat, well into the next century.

While some biologists are looking at genetic weakening as a problem resulting from interbreeding of various pheasant strains, others, like Wooley, feel that the hybridization has added vigor to the birds. Wooley falls squarely into the habitat-destruction camp in explaining pheasant shortages. My impression is that he's dead right, and all the other brouhahas amount largely to looking for ghosts in the closet.

One of the touchiest subjects having to do with pheasant hunting is the shooting of hens. Even though in captivity a rooster pheasant can breed with up to 30 hens, in the wild one rooster for three or four hens is the norm. This means that protecting hens—all hens—doesn't mean that they will all be bred and will rear chicks. Wooley reports that in some western states where hens have been included in the daily bag, to his knowledge there have been no detrimental effects on the overall population.

With many other gallinaceous birds, like ruffed grouse, there is no easy way to identify a female in flight, as there is with pheasants. Therefore the females of those species are legal targets. However, with pheasants, the hens are readily distinguishable from the cockbirds, so it's easy to protect them, thinking that we are saving breeders.

However, if habitat is the key, then survival should be

assured through proper habitat even if hens are included in the daily bag. A study done in the 1960s indicated that hen harvest had no detrimental effect on the population until it surpassed 25% of the total kill. In Iowa, according to Wooley, the illegal harvest of hens through poaching and mistakes is 9%—well within the parameters of the 25% harvest limit.

Does it make sense to harvest hens, especially when we know many will go unbred in the spring? First, I think that in order to make hen harvest work, the modern pheasant hunter would have to get over his aversion to shooting a lady bird—it seems cruel somehow, and I admit I'd have to swallow hard before I dropped the hammer on a hen. I think we're dealing with the same set of problems that arise when does are allowed during deer seasons: the idea is biologically sound but unpopular.

But again, if the habitat gains expected under the Farm Bill come about, increasing the shooting opportunities by introducing hens as legal targets is a moot point. There ought to be enough roosters to go around.

Here's a Farm Bill rundown, according to a U.S. government publication:

"The *conservation section* includes new programs to protect fragile soils and wetlands for future generations and move a substantial amount of erodible land into less intensive use.

"For highly erodible land which has not been cultivated since 1980, the bill provides a 'sodbuster' program to discourage plowing up fragile soils. If a farmer planted a crop on fragile land in violation of the terms of the bill, he would lose price supports and other farm benefits for *all* of his crops in the year of the violation. Highly erodible land which was used for crops (or idled under a government acreage control program) between 1981 and 1985 would initially be exempt from the sodbuster penalties, but this 'grandfather clause' exemption would disappear for any affected producer who fails to begin applying a conservation plan by 1990 or two years after completion of a soil survey

A pheasant management area. It has been found that such areas receive their highest usage by birds during the winter months, when cover on neighboring farms has been flattened by harvest and weather. Then management areas pull birds in from as far as several miles away.

of his land, whichever is later. Producers would have until 1995 to complete application of the benefits to producers who convert wetlands to crop use in the future, except in cases where the impact of the action is found to be minimal.

"For highly erodible soils which are already in crop use, the bill provides a long-term Conservation Reserve program under which farmers would contract for periods of 10 to 15 years to return 40 to 45 million of such acres to less-intensive uses such as grass or trees, which in some cases may be used to establish shelterbelts. In return for compliance with the contracts, growers would get cash or in-kind land rental payments (established on a bid basis) plus payments covering a part of the cost of needed land-treatment measures. No more than 25 percent of the land in any county could be enrolled in the Reserve, except in counties where the Secretary of Agriculture decides that higher levels would not hurt the county economy. There would be a $50,000 limit on annual payments to farmers under Reserve contracts.

"Also, the bill includes an extension of the Resources Conservation Act, requiring the Agriculture Department to produce assessments of soil and water resources in 1995 and again in 2005 to help policymakers develop long-term plans for protecting those vital national resources. A further section permits governors of states which have state laws to protect farmland from urban development to file suits in cases where the federal government has not followed procedures of a federal farmland protection law. (The federal law requires, among other points, that government agencies must consider alternatives before taking actions which result in shifting farmland to nonfarm use.)

"The bill requires the Secretary of Agriculture to establish a procedure under which adverse determinations made under these new conservation provisions may be appealed.

"The bill authorizes the Secretary of Agriculture to formulate plans and give technical assistance to property owners, state and local agencies, and interstate river basin commissions to protect the quality and quantity of subsurface water, reduce flooding hazards, and control salinity. The Secretary must report to Congress on this matter by February 15, 1987."

So we are going to have to lobby, write letters, and join forces to make sure that the Farm Bill stays the law of the land. Will it take some extra money? How's about a $5 Federal Pheasant stamp with the proceeds going to help fund the Conservation Reserve section of the Farm Bill? I've got no problem with that.

Should we join Pheasants Forever and use that organization as a motivating force to keep what's been won and looks so good, at least on paper? Youbetcherlife.

I'm guessing now, but I would say that some farms in the Midwest would be a whole lot better off as pheasant-hunting havens for out-of-state shooters than as functioning farms. With the Farm Bill's provisions, and with up to 25% of the land of any one county set aside for what could end up being pheasant habitat, a couple of farms could, if they combined their acreage, serve as a nice base of operations for out-of-staters and resident hunters, too. Perhaps many farmers will come to the conclusion that pheasants and other wildlife grown on their places are a more marketable commodity than soybeans or corn or sugar beets, and that they should take advantage of the wildlife economically— nothing in the Farm Bill prevents it, by the way.

A couple of hunters put up a rooster at the edge of a cornfield. Small fields like this, devoted to rowcrop production, can provide excellent habitat when interspersed with windbreaks, woodlots, and various kinds of weedy or brushy edge cover. Enormous single-crop agribusiness fields, on the other hand, can be extremely detrimental. (Joe Workosky photo)

In this way then, farmers, the government through its tax systems, hunters, and local communities all have a vested interest in making sure that the program and the incentives continue, because everybody benefits. I'm only dreaming now, but it seems nice to know that we're getting some land for the birds.

As in the Soil Bank days, the economic incentives are there for farmers to participate in this broad-scale program. It is what pheasants—and ducks, woodcock, grouse, etc.— have needed for a long time: an economically viable reason for private landowners to set acreage aside and help it produce wildlife.

Let's say that this program works. Let's say that—just this once—the Feds know what they're doing and the parts of the United States which we call the Farm Belt, the pheasant belt, go for the Farm Bill provisions in a big way. Let's say we get 5 million acres the first year and more later. Then what?

Well, I think we're going to see a return to the days of yore. Maybe even better. In the last quarter century, most of us have accrued more leisure time and today we have more money—well, maybe *you* do! Additionally, a whole generation of pheasant hunters has gotten out of the game altogether. We all know people who gunned in the '40s, '50s, and '60s but put the Model 12 in the closet once the birds got scarce. Those people are going to come back out into the fields, the swamps, and the coverts in force, and we bird hunters are again going to be a political force to be reckoned with—a voting bloc of politically savvy shooters who know that it was a government program that got us this great opportunity and we don't want to give it up.

By the way, the Farm Bill's provisions call for quite a bit of acreage to be set aside in "trees," which offers hope for grouse and woodcock hunters as well—young forests are their prime habitat. We'll have to wait and see, I guess, but one of the things I look for the Farm Bill to do is lure more people back to pheasant hunting because of rising bird populations, thus taking some of the pressure off other species.

I know, for example, that most grouse hunters in my home state of Michigan would not be grouse hunters at all if there were enough pheasants to keep them interested.

Still another possibility exists—that dedicated hunters and farmers may wish to go for the establishment of pheasant food plots and other habitat under the provisions of the Farm Bill. With pheasants specifically in mind, here is some information provided by the Minnesota DNR's Section of Wildlife concerning pheasant food plots.

SORGHUM PLANTINGS FOR PHEASANTS—A way to create a pheasant wintering area in just one growing season. Designed for use on set-aside acres or other lands taken out of production under U.S. Department of Agriculture farm programs and one of the most useful and feasible ways to get pheasant cover on private lands. These plots provide both food and cover through the use of two different sorghum varieties. Grain-sorghum that grows to a height of about two feet provides the food and some cover. Cane-sorghum that grows to a height of about seven feet provides the dense cover. The cover provided by a sorghum plot resembles that of a cattail or canegrass marsh, and the birds love it.

VALUE—Cattail marshes have always been a winter cover preferred by the birds in Minnesota's prime pheasant range. We generally have our best pheasant populations where such cover is still available. Marsh cover provides a warm micro-climate and relative security from avian predation and harassment.

On the minus side, marshes can and do fill in with snow during severe blizzards, sometimes trapping and killing the birds. During severe prairie blizzards there is no cover that will protect the birds completely. Marshes or marsh-type cover are what the birds prefer, and help bring the birds through most winters.

Sorghum plots are a way of creating this marsh-type cover on upland sites.

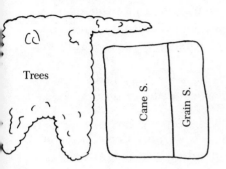

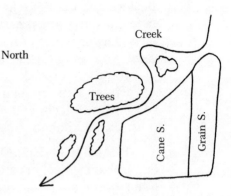

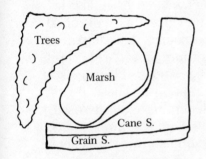

This drawing shows some suggested plantings for pheasant habitat. Such plantings could become both commonplace and highly productive under the provisions of the 1985 Farm Bill. (Minnesota DNR, Section of Wildlife.)

WINTERING AREAS—The primary purpose for sorghum plots is to create wintering areas with both food and cover for pheasants. The plots are left standing and unharvested over the winter months. Deer, rabbits, and other wildlife also make extensive use of such plantings.

NESTING COVER—Sorghum plots can also provide nesting cover. This is accomplished by not working up the plot the following spring, but instead waiting until August 1.

Besides gaining the extra wildlife use, this timing also eliminates any rush or pressure to clean up the plot during the
busy spring period. Most landowners will simply enroll the
same site as set-aside acres and rotate the new sorghum
plot to other set-aside acres.

Thus, with one planting it is possible to provide winter
cover, winter food, and nesting cover for pheasants . . . their
most critical habitat needs.

PLANTING DETAILS—*Site.* Sorghum does best on
dry upland sites. Locating the planting south and east of
other cover such as trees or a marsh helps keep blowing
snow out of the plot.

Size. A typical planting is 10 acres in size. The cane-
sorghum is planted to provide six acres of cover similar to a
cattail marsh. The grain-sorghum provides four acres of additional cover and the primary food source. It is important
not to exceed five acres of grain-sorghum on set-aside acres,
in order to comply with USDA regulations. Planting size
can be varied to adapt to local conditions. (These regulations can vary according to what federal program is used.)

Planting Time. The best time to plant sorghum is about
the first 10 days in June. The soil temperature must be 60°
F or higher. This is one of the most important requirements
for a successful planting. The relatively late planting date
allows for earlier sprouting weeds and grasses to be destroyed during seed-bed preparation. It is usually best to
plant the two sorghum varieties in separate plots.

Planting Rates. The cane-sorghum is planted at the
rate of eight or nine pounds of seed per acre. The grain-
sorghum is planted at a rate of six or seven pounds of seed
per acre. The sorghum seed comes in 50-pound sacks. A
sack of each variety is ample for a 10-acre planting.

Planting Machinery. The sorghum seed can be planted
with a grain drill or a corn planter. If a drill is used, at least
every other and probably two out of three openings must be
plugged. If a corn planter is used, the proper plates recommended by the manufacturer must be used. If the cane-
sorghum is planted with a corn planter, it is necessary to

double-plant. In that way you end up with 15-inch rows from a 30-inch planter.

Plot Cleanup. Some prefer to disk the plot very lightly, just enough to knock it down. Then burn it. It will burn and clean up nicely if it has been knocked down first. Others prefer to go over the plot with a stock chopper before working it up.

Recommended Varieties. Varieties that have worked well are Pioneer #877F (replaces #988) and Pioneer #931 for the cane-sorghum. Pioneer #894 works well for the grain-sorghum.

II
THE DOGS

My dog sleeps on the couch, sheds on the carpets, and minds me when she feels like it, which isn't often. But she can find, point, and hold pheasants. I like her better than I like most people.

Once, while hunting some brushy draws, I scratched down a rooster with a long shot. The bird hit the ground, righted himself immediately, and headed across a picked bean field toward some standing corn, my dog and I in hot pursuit. Making the corn, a 20-acre strip, the bird showed there was nothing wrong with his legs, and we never did get him, although the dog came close a couple of times.

The next day, a farmer friend called to tell me that he had been harvesting the field that day when he spotted a

A dog that will locate downed birds is of primary importance in pheasant hunting. My setter Jess will find birds . . .

and retrieve them to hand, but she doesn't like fetching very much, owing to a bad spurring during her first season. Like many pheasant dogs, she has a habit of bringing birds in dead. Somewhere in the scramble, she kills cripped birds, although the marks on them are minimal. Probably she breaks their necks with a well-placed bite and shake, not uncommon for aggressive dogs.

rooster that wouldn't run, so he stopped the combine, hopped off, and caught the bird, which had evidently lost a lot of its vitality. It always makes you feel good when a cripple is recovered, even if somebody else eats him.

My dog's a setter; if I'd had a Lab or a springer, I'd have had that bird.

I'm a rabid pointing-dog man, so it hurts like hell to say this, but the best pheasant dogs for today's shooting are the flushing breeds. The reason are simple—the habits and habitat of the bird. A rooster pheasant doesn't lie well for a pointing dog; rarely do we get an intense, locked-up point in the open with a setter or some other pointing breed. Instead, especially where bird numbers are low, the beggars run and the best we can get is a stiff-legged shuffle while the bird is streaking yards ahead.

A springer or a game-trained Labrador or golden retriever makes a much better pheasant dog because it stays with the birds and roots them out and into the air. And in the case of the retrievers, once the birds are down, they usually aren't going anywhere—the dog's going to get them.

A crippled cockbird is tough on a dog bred for and used on quail, ruffed grouse, and woodcock. I've had good dogs ruined as retrievers after they've mixed it up with a wing-tipped rooster who had nothing wrong with his spurs. You should see what a dog that kills roosters before fetching does to a lightly hit woodcock.

In Iowa one year, my son and I each drove shot into a low-flying rooster, and the bird came down hit hard but with his head up. My setter Jess was there in an instant, but the bird was gone. In that thick marsh grass it couldn't have gone far, and she kept pointing straight down. I thought she was pointing the scent where the bird had landed, but after feeling the matted grass, I picked up the bird—stone dead. With its last seconds of life, it had burrowed under the grass to die.

Such a feat is something of a record for my setter, but for a Lab, it's second nature. One time my dad shot a bird that hit the ground running, and the Lab we were using

"There's one in there somewhere," and indeed there was. The dog is
holding point while the hunters try to root out a dug-in bird. They did,
but it was a hen.

took off after it. We stood by the fencerow where the action
had occurred for maybe 15 minutes, and finally the dog's
owner pointed at a distant hill. Here came the dog—a half
mile off—with the bird in her mouth. You can't beat that
kind of performance. Getting a shot is tough, but getting the
bird in hand afterward can be tougher, because *they're*
tough.

A flushing dog closely simulates the hunting sounds
and movements of the ground-based predators that pheasants have to deal with: raccoons, foxes, coyotes, and so
forth. Such predators are real bulldogs when it comes to
getting the scent of a bird and following it to its source.

The pheasant, realizing that he could get caught, waits
until the predator (the flushing dog) is nearly upon him and
then uses his final option: flight. He won't go any sooner
than he has to, but when the ground-bound predator gets
close enough, he'll flush, and that's what you want.

Years ago I watched a red fox working through a wheat-stubble field in the early morning. He was trailing and sniffing and stalking and chasing something. As he became more excited, I saw a pheasant head pop up about 20 yards ahead, and then the head dropped and the bird doubled back around the fox. But the little guy was not easily dissuaded. He kept on the trail and followed the bird for another 30 or 35 yards. The bird finally flushed when the fox got within about 10 yards. The fox watched, seemed to shrug his shoulders, and sauntered away to look for mice. The lesson is this: with a flushing dog, instead of a fox, that bird could have been in a hunter's bag.

Whenever you use a flushing dog—or any dog, in fact—it's best to remain quiet. Don't talk at all if you can avoid it. Pheasants will get a fix on your position from your voice and will flush away from you. You want the birds to think the contest is between your dog and them—you're not a factor.

A flushing dog—be it a springer, an English cocker (which is making a comeback as a hunting breed), or a game-trained retriever—should know some basic commands. Obviously, the yard-training commands of "sit," "stay," "come," "heel," and so forth are important, but a dog should also know hand signals, directions given by a wave of the hand. Those signals are best taught in an open field by making a throwing motion with your hand in the direction you want the dog to head, and then taking a series of huge steps in that direction. The dog, in staying in front of you, will gravitate that way. Work the dog on hand signals, changing directions across a field and gradually moving into thicker and thicker cover, for 15 minutes a day until a wave of the hand will send him where you want him to go. Your dog, viewing the world from a low vantage point, can't always see the best cover to be worked; you can, and can wave him there.

The dog should also be steady to wing and steady to shot. These terms, often misunderstood, simply mean the dog, once the bird is in the air, shouldn't be part of the action until you want him to be. A spaniel or Lab should "hup" when a bird goes out; he should simply sit at the spot where the bird flushed, watching it. At the shot, the dog should remain sitting until he is given the command to "fetch" or "hunt dead." In thick cover, the combination of a slow-rising rooster and a jumping dog can have disastrous consequences if the shot is too quick. Some dogs can leap pretty high, and every year a few leap right into a shot pattern. At the very least, such a dog is made gunshy; at worst, well . . .

The Labrador retriever is one of the top pheasant breeds. Working as a flusher in the manner of a springer spaniel, the Lab is the best bet for finding downed birds. Here a wet dog and a wet hunter bagged a wet rooster pheasant and a late-flighting woodcock. Both birds came from permanent, streamside cover.

"Hunting dead" can be taught with food, and the teaching should begin very early. I like to use pieces of weenies that I have spread out in high grass. I take the dog into the area, and, making a circular motion with my hand, palm down, I croon, "Dead bird." The pup stumbles upon a hot dog and eats it (later on you can easily make sure he doesn't eat birds). After a few passes, a puppy learns that the phrase and the gesture mean there's something in the grass right here that he ought to know about because it's good.

Pigeons that have been shot can be placed and found in the same way, making the transition from Oscar Mayer to birds easier.

Pointing breeds should know hand signals as well, and they should be steady to wing and shot. Also, they should have the knack of holding a point, but should still be able to handle a running bird. My setter has lately taken to racing ahead and pinning running roosters by heading them off, and it's pretty to see. I've seen other dogs do this as well. She learned the trick on running ruffed grouse and adapted it to ringnecks. But—and it's a big but—they don't stay pinned long for her or any other dogs I've seen do it, and if the bird is in sparse cover when it happens, it will flush immediately, sometimes with the gunner 100 yards away. Apparently, the circling maneuver by the dog convinces the bird that there are two dogs (or foxes or coyotes or whatever), and it either freezes to hide in thick cover or takes wing on the spot in open stuff. In either case, you have to be there. Dogs that do this are fun to hunt with, but it's a trick they have to learn themselves, and it takes a sharp cookie to learn it. The flushing breeds, on the other hand, just do what comes naturally.

In many of the places pheasants inhabit, especially in the East, thick cover in tiny pockets is the rule. If a pointing dog goes in and locks up, you have to go in to flush, often making a shot impossible. A flushing dog, by contrast, will plow through the cover, pushing any birds out to you as you stand ready in a good vantage point.

My pal Chuck Lichon and his fat Lab Jill have a nice

Among the pointing breeds, the Continental, short-tailed dogs are considered by many to be tops for pheasants. This German shorthair helped his
hunter take an early-season preserve bird. Shooting preserves offer a
chance for both dog and hunter to get in trim before the season—and
they extend shooting past the normal state seasons. (Joe Workosky
photo)

system: Charlie places the dog on sit on one side of a piece
of cover while he silently circles and waits at the other side.
He then gives a low whistle, and Jill starts through. Any
birds rousted out go away from the dog and toward Charlie,
who then misses them because he's a lousy shot—but it's a
good scam.

A puppy picked as a pheasant dog should be one that

exhibits early the aggressiveness this sport needs in an animal. The dominant pup in a litter of average-temperament parents is a good bet. Above all, stay away from a shy or "sweet" little pup. You want the one that's eating your shoelaces or biting your ankles when you look the litter over. A pheasant dog has to have moxie—period!

Maybe it doesn't belong here, but I'll tell you anyway so that you can help justify the price of this book. Some dogs will go gunshy on you. It's something that each dog man fears, and so we take the usual preventive measures as the dogs are growing—we bang pans at feeding time and fire cap pistols and .22s and so forth. But eventually you'll run into one that has the malady. Actual gunshyness is rare and is often inherited. What it should be called is "gun nervousness." How it starts—perhaps the result of some overenthusiastic shooting during early training sessions—really doesn't matter once the problem hits.

Jess, my setter, got gun-nervous on me in her first year. I was heartsick. I mean, I love that dog, and I saw a bunch of good years ahead. Well, I consulted everyone I knew, and everybody said basically, "Hell, I don't know."

So I worked out the scheme that follows. I let everything she did that was fun or tasted good become associated with loud noises. Jess is a real beggar—like most setters, she'll eat all the time if you let her. In the kitchen is a cupboard that holds her doggie treats. While she was out of the room, I'd slam the cupboard door and call her. When she came, I'd give her a treat. I did this for a week, four or five times a day. After awhile I didn't have to call her—I just slammed the door, and I mean *slammed* (I broke it twice). I have a large kitchen, so the sound really echoed. No matter where she was, she knew that sound meant a biscuit, and she was there.

Then I got myself a cap pistol (by the way, they really make cap pistols cheaply these days) and stuffed my pockets with treats. I walked around the house two or three times a day, popping off my caps and giving her the treats every time she came, praising her all the time.

Author teaches "Whoa!" to his setter as a young dog. Notice that the check cord is in use and the dog is giving her undivided attention. The teaching of basic commands—"come," "sit," "stay," "heel," "whoa," and so forth—is essential to any pointing dog, but seems even more important for pheasant hunting, when running birds and strong scent can confuse a dog.

Next it was the same maneuver with a blank-firing training pistol; same results. Jess also likes to ride in the car, so I'd use the pistol to call her from the yard or house to the car in the driveway. We'd go for a little ride while she munched on biscuits.

The next season, when a bird flushed and I shot, she never even noticed the sound. I used a long-barreled 20 gauge that first year because the report is so much less than that of a short-barreled 12. Now I use the 12 with no problem.

Jess still hates the neighbor kids' firecrackers and she quivers in a thunderstorm, but she's not gunshy anymore.

What dog is "best" depends on your hunting habits. I've seen preserve dogs that knew their job by rote, going from patch to patch almost by memory and pushing birds into the air. I've seen farm mutts with three legs that would have given the best springer that ever lived a go in a head-to-head pheasant-finding competition.

One fellow I know—and I've heard similar reports from others—runs his Pennsylvania ringnecks with a beagle; claims the dog yowls differently on a pheasant than on a rabbit—I wonder how many circles the dog ran before he figured out the difference.

I had a pointer once that was a pheasant-hunting machine. He held birds, lived to hunt, and was a canine athlete. Before a car took his life, I wondered what to do with him the 10 months of the year I wasn't hunting—he was that hot. Remember, before you buy a pup, you'll be living with it *all* year. The dog should have a personality you'll enjoy during the nonhunting months.

Of all the faults that give dog men the vapors, none is worse than the dog that hunts way off, working at two shotgun ranges away, or one that takes off on a beeline for the next area code, busting through good cover en route.

The electronic collar is a Godsend for hardheads like this. It allows you to give him a touch of juice along with a "NO!" hollered with all the plugs out. A dog that's been flipped over by the electric collar a couple of times learns that if he stays close and hunts like a good boy, the zipper won't get him.

The typical scenario goes like this: Dog takes off with collar in place. Owner, who has been savoring this moment, calls the dog back, but of course, it ignores him like he's dust. At 80 yards, Owner screams at the dog and hits the button. *Whack!* Judgment day. Owner calls the dog in and tells him, "Yes, little Sport, I know—the Boogie Man got you. But if you stay here with me, you'll be safe." The funny thing is, the dog comes to believe it.

The collar as a fault-correction device is great. As a punishment tool it's misused. I've seen guys get the same look on their faces they'd have if they got one good pop at the Ayatollah—evil glee—just before they zapped a pooch. In such cases, they are not training, they are getting even.

A happy little springer spaniel courses an eastern woodlot looking for pheasants. The springer is the No. 1 pheasant specialist, and dogs of this breed with a lot of aggressiveness are preferred; they have the dash and fire to get on a running bird quickly and force it into the air. With a hesitant dog of any breed, the bird has time to make tracks and then flush wild. The springer, when properly trained, will root birds into the air and then "hup" (sit) until after the shot. And it will retrieve on command. Today some hunters are having good luck with the slightly smaller English cocker spaniel. Both breeds make good house pets and buddies during the 10 months or more of the year you *don't* hunt. (Tom Carney photo)

Still, it does the heart good to see an arrogant, ill-mannered mutt get a well-deserved punishment.

If I were to bring a pup along—and I probably will

before too long—I'd start the dog with the noise regimen to avoid gunshyness. Then, as he got older, I'd work on the yard commands of "sit," "stay," and "come." A young pointing dog would get a look at a bird wing on a stick to show him pointing is fun and that I like him when he does it.

Next we would go into the field for quartering development and hand signals, and then work on planted pigeons. I would let him flush or point the first few pigeons; then I'd shoot a few.

After that, we'd head for a shooting preserve for work on pheasants. All this time, the dog would never be off a check cord—plastic clothesline slides nicely through cover.

A pal, Tom Carney, has a nice little male setter named Paddy. I went to a preserve with Tom and Paddy to give Tom a hand. The dog was rushing in on point and then chasing the flushed bird. Tom, a nice man who loves his dog, was coming unglued, and so I came along to try to help.

When Paddy pointed a planted bird, I took the check cord—which Paddy wasn't used to—and held him back while Tom yelled "Whoa!" Then the bird was flushed, and we let it fly off. Paddy took off like Secretariat on a dry track. I waited until the cord got to the end; then I yanked. Paddy is a small setter, the cord was strong, and I had a point to prove.

When he got off his back and blinked back the tears, Paddy came in and seemed to ask Tom if he thought maybe chasing birds was a poor idea. End of problem. A smart dog, Paddy wised up quickly. The point is that sometimes we need outside help in dog training because so much of it takes two men, and sometimes you don't have the heart to give your own dog the stern treatment he needs.

After you've shot a few birds—pigeons or preserve birds—over your pup, don't shoot any more until the dog does everything right. He has to learn he won't get that bird unless he does it by the numbers. And always have the check cord in hand so that you are in control. If you have someone else out there to shoot the birds, make sure that

The Irish setter, whose heyday has passed, still retains popularity among some hunters and may be making a comeback. Breeding for the show ring and bench has removed much of the hunting fire from the breed, but strains are still being bred like the reds of old. (MI DNR photo)

Dave Meisner, founder of *Gun Dog* magazine, accepts an Iowa rooster from Max, his German wirehair. Most wirehair owners may be thankful for the saying that beauty is only skin-deep, but they also like to stress that beauty is as beauty does. This versatile breed just may be the best of all pointing dogs on pheasants. (Dave Meisner photo)

the helper understands that this is *dog* training, not *shooter* training, and will fire only when you say so.

A pheasant dog has to be under control all the time. There are places where the scent can be downright thick. In such conditions a dog can come apart and start chasing. Then comes the whistling, the screaming, and the swearing, and the birds become specks on the horizon. A dog not able to control himself has to be worked—with you alone— until he can.

Personally, I prefer a pointing dog, but they have drawbacks, especially if they're not staunch. A dog trained to hold his points on woodcock and quail can find it unnerving to lock up on hot scent and have the owner—knowing the bird is hotfooting it over the next rise 100 yards away— screaming at him to break point and relocate. It's then tough to get the dog shifted back to woodcock or quail and have all things mannerly. Something's going to break down, and unless you're a pheasant specialist or use a dog as a specialist, you may have problems. Some dogs can switch gears; others can't. The most effective—not necessarily the most stylish—of the pointing breeds turn into semi-flushers after long years on ringnecks.

That's what I like about the so-called "versatile" breeds—wirehairs, Griffons, pudelpointers, the short-tailed European breeds—they do what they have to do to get you birds. A good wirehair, for example, will point, retrieve (even in water), ground trail, and do everything else that's required. Those breeds may not point with the intensity of a pointer, or fetch like a Lab, or ground trail a winged bird like a springer, but for a *package* of skills, you just can't beat them.

Pheasant hunting is rough on dogs. The distances are long in terms of ground covered, the cover is usually pretty rugged, and the birds themselves are tough.

It makes sense to carry a first-aid kit for dogs. Some on the market are pretty good, or you may choose to make up one of your own. I've got one of each, so I'll make a list of the stuff you should have in it. This is a basic kit, and you may want to include more items:

white medical adhesive tape

hemostats

gauze (pads and roll)

elastic bandage

eye ointment

antiseptic (ointment or liquid)

needle-nosed pliers or forceps

needle and thread

sulfa powder ("Sulfacaine")

chemical cooling pack (cools when contents are squeezed and mixed)

Band-aids

small razor blade or scalpel

The author styles up a young pointer on training pigeons prior to his first season. It can't hurt—and the use of pigeons can help considerably in training quail dogs—but only pheasants will make a good pheasant dog. (Dave Meisner photo)

Most of the wear and tear on a dog comes around the eyes, nose, and ears, so look for cuts there. A healthy dog is a quick healer, but you still should call the animal in and look him over periodically. An eager hunter will often ignore minor wounds that can cause problems later on. Rest the dog, and check him out.

III
THE HUNT

When biologists need to handle any given gamebird, they immobilize it by grabbing the appendages that bird uses the most and has the most confidence in. To keep a duck still, you grab his wings. To keep a pheasant still, you hold his legs. Hmmmmmmm.

When most of us first picked up a shotgun, we probably learned from our father or an interested uncle that pheasants were the gamebirds favored by most Americans. We may have spent our early years shooting at ruffed grouse or woodcock or maybe even quail, but when push came to shove, it was a rooster pheasant that we wanted over our gun barrel.

Many of us drifted off to the pursuit of other birds. But

Hunting fields such as this is normally a waste of time. However, this early-morning hunter managed to catch a laggard before the bird walked or flew to feed. Hunting roosting cover can be productive, provided the cover is thick enough, such as waist-high foxtail or other grasses. As the season progresses, birds tend to stay in the roosting cover longer, until the grass dries a bit from overnight frosts. Overcast days also delay their movement a bit.

pheasants still draw us. And plenty of pheasants are still out there for the shooting, but most of us need to adapt our tactics to the conditions and to the birds of this decade.

When most of us were younger, it was the standard technique of driving cropfields that put pheasants in the air. We took turns driving and standing and waiting for the roosters to come out to us. No more, however, and there are a few good reasons.

First off, crops are now expensive to grow. The hybrid corn and soybeans grown from registered seed mean a lot of money to a farmer, enough so that he has no urge to let a bunch of strangers traipse through them.

Rowcrops like standing corn tend to scatter birds and also make it almost impossible to get them into the air. The scent conditions and lack of ground cover in a cornfield are likely to drive your dog crazy, too, turning the hunt into a footrace between hunters, dogs, and scurrying birds. This situation is dangerous at best.

Hunting is a lot safer and more productive in permanent cover. Throughout pheasant range you'll find farms with woodlots, sloughs, ditches, and all sorts of standing cover that has been left alone. It is here that you'll find pheasants, if they're around, and it is here that you'll have a fighting chance.

Such hunting more closely resembles ruffed grouse hunting, or maybe even rough-country quail shooting. The tactics that work for grouse will work for pheasants: two or three people and a dog working small patches slowly, getting birds into the air when they have run out of the last of the cover. True, grouse will hold better for a dog, but the pheasant hunter must be cognizant that birds will run ahead of him. So it's imperative that he work woodlots and brushy patches *away* from other cover and *toward* open ground where the birds will have to fly. The action will come on the edges.

Pheasant hunting success today depends largely upon conditions. A windy day is actually good for hunting—if you hunt into the wind. True, the birds are more skittish, but the wind also masks your sound and better carries the birds' scent to your dog, putting the odds a bit more in your favor. On rainy days the birds hold better and scenting is better—unless there's a downpour.

Small patches of cover are the places for small parties—two to four hunters and a dog or two. Fencerows, ditch banks, field terraces—these permanent strips of cover lend themselves to the block-and-drive technique on a small scale.

In a recent fall in Nebraska, I was hunting with my father and my son. I was handling the dog, and we were hunting the thick cover along a ditch bank. The strip was about 50 yards wide. My setter was pointing and then breaking, so I knew that birds were running ahead. I stopped and motioned the other two in wide circles around the cover strip to its end, where they stood as standers, and then I started through. Sure enough, two roosters jumped 100 yards in front of me, but right in front of the silent standers, and they dropped them both. I'm convinced such tactics work if you're quiet and careful.

Small drives can work well. One fall I was hunting gullies in Iowa, waste places that tapered up into plowed fields. The fingers of the guillies fanned out like the fingers of a hand, each of the fingers being 35-50 yards long and emanating from a center section about 100 yards in diameter. One by one I worked the fingers, pushing what I hoped were running birds toward the open, but moving very quietly and slowly. I shot two roosters, one at the end of each of the first two fingers, and flushed several other birds, mostly hens. The point is that working alone—just with my dog—I got good shooting because I pushed the birds to where they didn't want to go. Had I had a partner, I'm sure that even some of the wild flushers would have been in the bag because I would have stationed my companion at the end of each finger and pinched the birds: that's the block-and-drive method.

With pheasants, you must work each patch of cover right to the end, assuming that there is a bird which will not move until you've walked through the last square yard of cover. It happens often enough that I'm convinced that stopping 10 feet short of the open won't push some birds out—they have to be rooted out.

Naturally, some birds will hold in the middle of a cover

Late in the season, roosters like to seek out thick cover such as this second-growth woodlot that has been sheltered from the wind by pine trees. When cover is depleted because of weather, birds are often reluctant to leave it. Such pieces of thick cover should be approached *into* the wind to give dogs a chance to flush or point any birds present, and also to muffle the sound of your approach.

patch, but they are rare. I find that the best time to hunt is early in the season in roosting cover, just at the start of legal shooting time. I've enjoyed some good dog work by hitting such places first. Later on in the day and in the season, the birds don't cooperate as well.

As a season progresses, the pheasants will move into the corn and will stay until it's harvested; then they will head for the thick stuff, and the thicker, the better. Among the most overlooked places are wet areas—places that have standing water most of the year, hold marsh grasses, and are generally difficult to move around in. When pressure gets heavy, the birds will head for these areas because they're less likely to be disturbed there by predators, either four-footed or two-footed.

In the East, cattail sloughs offer good sport, especially on the small, dry islands or hummocks that dot large sloughs. On farms, the inevitable low, brushy spots are safe refuges for pheasants pushed from more traditional cover by gun presusre. As crop harvest and weather flatten standing cover, such places become gold mines in years of good bird populations; after freeze-up in states offering late shooting, they are the *only* way to go—hunt them first. The birds will use these places for roosting and resting, venturing out briefly to feed only in the late morning and again in the afternoon.

Jim Marti, a friend of mine who owns and operates the Burnt Creek Kennels in North Dakota, told me about a hunting method he uses on ringnecks in small to moderate-sized fields. He will use two dogs, one a big-going dog—a real smoker—and the other an animal that's much more biddable, a dog that you can even keep at heel. Jim collars the wide-ranging dog with a big bell, one that will really clang, and turns him loose in the corn. With the other dog under tight control, he sneaks into the field very quietly. Now, the wide-running dog is in there chasing pheasants and having a grand old time. But because of the bell, the birds know exactly where he is, so they circle to avoid him. What you have now is a situation in which birds are milling around, running and sneaking across the hither and yon, doing their level best to stay away from something that sounds like an angel-dusted reindeer. Thus distracted, they are easy marks for the slow-moving Marti and his adroit, closer-working dog.

Jim says that birds pinned this way stay put as if glued. He also says that a flushing dog will do just as well in this situation. The confused pheasants will sit tight or flush from underfoot under such circumstances; he just gives them something to think about—the dog with the bell.

My setter totes a bell when we're grouse hunting, but

when we're after pheasants, I take the bell's clapper out. My psychotic dog won't hunt well unless she wears *her* collar and has *her* familiar bell banging her chest. The absence of a bell ringing doesn't matter—I guess she needs the "feel" to get into the mood.

Early-season pheasants are stupid—well, about as stupid as pheasants ever get. Mostly, they are the young-of-the-year birds that haven't encountered hunters before. These birds fly readily, comparatively speaking. They are easily confused, and if you get an old, experienced dog up against a brushy draw full of young, inexperienced roosters, you'll soon be back in the local diner having a late breakfast with your limit cooling in the trunk.

Statistically, the largest kill comes in the first hour of opening day. After that, the birds are wary and they scatter. Wild flushing becomes the rule of the day, and refugees head for standing cropfields to count survivors.

As the season progresses, the remaining birds are isolated and confined to existing cover, cover which wind, weather, and harvest continue to reduce. Hunting birds in the middle of the season becomes a matter of looking for cover which has in it, or nearby, food, water, and shelter. Water is a variable the birds can do without if pressure is heavy. Even readily available food can be scratched in areas of intensive hunting activity; never will they be far from protective cover.

Most of the pheasant states have areas managed specially for pheasants and other game. Opening day can find quite a horde of hunters on these spots, and the word gets out pretty quickly that such-and-such an area has been "shot out." As cover diminishes, that remains true—up to a point. Late in the season, usually after all the crops are in and snow is at least a possibility if not already on the ground, these areas will draw birds back to them. Now, most hunters will have long since crossed these spots off, but the pheasants are again using them because they're often the only thing around—the birds have no choice. So, late in the year, the smart money hits the managed areas

Tracking winter pheasants can be exciting sport. These tracks are close together and meandering, indicating an undisturbed bird. . .

and pushes the thickest stuff there is with a good dog. Pheasants taken this way qualify as trophy birds.

Like most people, I don't hunt pheasants as much as I'd like. The fact is, I do most of my pheasant hunting late in the season, doing very little early except for the opening-day festivities. And in the Plains States where the seasons normally open late, compared to the October openers common back East, the chances are good that snow will be present for much of the pheasant season.

I dearly love to hunt in snow because the birds are a bit easier to find. By looking for the pockets described in this

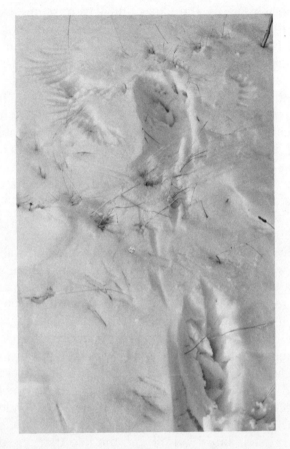

but often this is what the tracker finds at the end of his hunt: the marks
left by a bird that detected him and flushed before he was close enough
for a shot.

book, you can have good late-season shooting. Besides, the
timid souls all head indoors once the chill factor hits 30
below. Bunchasissies.

Hunting in the snow is a treat, one that can be very
productive. It's also educational as hell. Snow hunting
means pushing isolated habitat. In many ways, it's like big-
game hunting, where stalking potential holding areas pays
off. Let me explain.

Last winter my son Chris and I were doing some late-season hunting. About four inches of soft snow was on the ground when we flushed a wild rooster out of range. The bird pitched into a woodlot, and we hiked on over to see who was home. About 100 feet into the woodlot, I found where the bird had landed. Keeping the dog at heel, we started tracking the pheasant. We could see where the bird's long tail dragged in the snow as he ambled and weaved between trees; we saw where he dashed across openings, the snow heavily disturbed and the tracks well spaced; we saw where he had turned to watch us cross an opening and how he had made a sharp turn to try to lose us; we saw where he thought about sitting tight in a clump of grass, hoping we'd walk by.

It was really fun, but eventually the inevitable happened: we got close enough, and he flushed. Since we were both watching the track, we managed only one shot—Chris' 20 gauge cracked like a .22 in the snow-muffled woods.

Again we watched as the bird sailed back to the first piece of cover. Again we followed, repeating all the maneuvers, except that this time the dog wouldn't stay at heel. She ran ahead, pointed, and then grabbed a dead rooster. The bird had two shot in the vitals. There had been no blood, no feathers, no indication he'd been hit. The snow allowed us to find him. It makes you shudder when you wonder how many "missed" birds sail off and die like that one did.

The late season also brings a peculiar flocking of pheasants, and they flock up more or less according to sex. Roosters hang out together like bighorn rams. Problem is, they hang out in some gawdawful places, the thickest they can find: cattails, blackberry canes, standing grass, old railroad rights-of-way (dandy places to hunt, by the way).

If you can find a concentration of roosters, it doesn't necessarily follow that you'll be in luck. The late-season bird is a crafty lad with ears like your mother-in-law, legs like a whitetail, eyes like a hawk, and given to dirty tricks.

Sometimes, for strange reasons, pheasants are reluctant to leave a good piece of cover, even when they are at a marked disadvantage. One late-season day in Nebraska, a pal and I and my son got into an area of downed trees and young, regenerating growth in a little bowl surrounded by conifers. The little piece of cover was no more than 10 acres, but it must have held two dozen birds—almost all roosters. The dog worked perfectly, and even with some shooting, many of the birds stayed put. We stayed until our limits were completed. The next day, a major ice storm made roads impassable. I think the birds sensed the oncoming storm and were reluctant to leave a sheltered place, out of the wind and all. Locating a honey-hole like that can make a trip for you.

Late-season hunting can give you such opportunities because the birds are bunched in available cover—and there isn't much available. Hit it right, and you'll never forget it.

Now here's a bit of advice you may find at least strange and at most disagreeable: the proper way to hunt late-season rooster pheasants, the way to give them their due so that you don't regularly get snookered, is to hunt them as though you were hunting people. That's right—*people.*

The problem that hunters have after opening morning is failing to realize just how smart a rooster gets and how fast he gets that way. Your average hunter does not give your average pheasant enough of what you might call average credit for being smart, and the birds—including the odd young one that somehow survived the opening-day fusillade and fell in with the old-timers that knew what they were doing—win their skirmishes with hunters.

So suppose you had a brushy draw that held rooster pheasants, and you wanted to approach so as to get them into the air within shotgun range—the essence of pheasant hunting. Well, how would you approach if they were people instead of birds?

First, you'd probably be very silent. You'd leave the car some distance away, and you'd walk the extra yards so as not to spook the quarry. Next, you'd use the wind to your advantage by keeping it in your face and in your dog's face.

The author with a rainy-day ringneck. Abandoned farmsteads often are the first areas to "come back" into pheasant habitat. Many times the crop-producing land continues to be planted, but the original owner's homestead is neglected. The resulting growth near crops can produce very good, two- and three-acre pockets of pheasant habitat. On rainy days, birds are reluctant to fly because of low-pressure air and wet feathers. At such times pointing dogs, like the author's setter Jess, are at their best. Additionally, scenting conditions are usually quite good, unless the rain is a downpour.

This tactic minimizes the transference of sound from you to the quarry and maximizes transference of the quarry's scent to your dog. Next, you'd probably cover all avenues of escape by placing people where the beggars are likely to run out, and you'd get your people there as quietly and unobtrusively as possible. You'd also work the cover so as to drive the quarry from dense cover toward open ground where it would have to take flight. And you'd do all this without talking, following a plan designed well ahead of time.

Never underestimate a pheasant's capacity to learn and

Woodlot pheasant hunting is common in most of the bird's eastern range. Here a dog has located a running bird in thick second-growth hardwoods. At such times the hunting—and the shooting—resemble ruffed grouse sport.

adapt. This is a creature that has been adapting to humans since before the redwoods grew. Give him some credit for smarts.

Above all, remember that good pheasant cover in good range almost always holds some birds. If you didn't get them up, it's because you didn't make enough tracks through the place. Make some more.

Birds that are pushed into the air out of range can often be relocated near where they've put down. A pheasant will often fly toward cover, land short of it, and then run into the thickest stuff, where he'll sit tight. Like any light-breasted bird, he would rather run than fly; flying is taxing on him compared with, say, a dark-breasted duck or dove. So if you push a rooster out and he flies a distance, go after him, and be ready where the cover thickens.

Terraces—steep areas between relatively level spots,

Author's son and father prepare to hunt a prairie railroad right-of-way. Notice that the tracks and crossties have been removed, but that the grade and its attendant cover remain. Such areas, crossing vast distances through cropland, tend to get better as the season progresses. Notice that the younger generation goes for a side-by-side double while the older generation stays with a time-tested Model 12 Winchester. The middle generation is taking the picture.

such as on many farm fields—are good, but normally they lack the really thick cover birds need for late-season survival, thus making them better early-season bets. But if the cover on a terrace has been there long enough to "brush up," then hunt it anytime. Terraces are best worked by two hunters and a dog, plus a blocker at the end. The blocker waits silently while the cover is thoroughly worked by the two men with the dog. The point is not to have all the birds driven to the stander, but rather to have someone within range when and if the birds go up out of range of the drivers.

Certain places seem to harbor birds more naturally than

others, usually the undisturbed spots. Railroad rights-of-way where there is good, permanent cover are among such spots. In the old days, before effective trucking developed, railroad spur lines led to every farm town in the pheasant's range. Now, in many places, the rails and ties have been pulled up and hauled away, but the old grade, the low gullies on either side—and the cover—remain.

These spur lines can be worked effectively by two hunters. Park your car some distance away from the hunting area, and send your partner ahead in a circular path about of 200 to 400 yards, depending on how thick the cover is—the thicker it is, the closer he can get to it. The partner goes right down into the gulley running parallel to the old grade. After he's in position, you and your dog work the gulley toward him. Any birds pinched between you will have no place to go and must flush. Without the blocker, though, the birds are free to run down the gulley forever.

Once you've reached your partner, send him on another circular path to the next blocking position—or switch off and you be the blocker—and take another chunk of the gulley. After three or four such leapfrog movements, cross the old grade and work the other gulley in the same manner back toward the car.

A variation of this is to use two cars. One person—or two, one in each gulley—stands and another, starting at the next mile road, works toward the blocker or blockers. Working very slowly, you could, potentially, have a mile's worth of pheasants pinched between you. Again, you must be silent. I've found that hunting such grades with two drivers, one in each gulley, and two blockers, one in each gulley, really does the trick. The birds can only run ahead until they hit the blockers. When all the action is over, the drivers and the blockers head for the blockers' car for a lift back to their own vehicle and head for another section of old RR grade.

A similar four-man, two-dog arrangement works well on long windrows or shelterbelts—thick tree and brush growth established in strips to stop erosion and block wind. Send

Good thinking: you may as well bypass standing corn—the birds will not
hold there, dogs don't work well in it, shooting in it can be dangerous,
and nothing short of a regiment can move birds out of it anyway. Besides, with the price of hybrid corn today, many farmers don't want
people in the fields. Better to hunt thick, permanent cover near such
fields.

two men ahead by car to block the end, one on each side,
while the drivers and their dogs work toward the others.

Patches of cover in farm fields are mini-goldmines.
Near my home there is a field that is often planted to corn.
Nearly in the middle of that field is a little slough about the
size of a living room. After the corn is picked each year, I
visit my little slough, and I almost always pick up a bird or
two. The birds are there. They roost in the slough and feed
in the corn. But before the corn is down, it's a waste of time
to go after them—they'd just run into the corn and be gone.
But after the crop is picked, they use the spot for cover,
slipping out to feed on grain shattered by the combines and
slipping back to while away the day. That's when I get 'em.

On the plains, plum thickets can offer the necessary

These hunters scored by workiing the brushy draws bordering this harvested cornfield. Mechanical pickers leave much grain smashed and
scattered, giving pheasants a ready food supply. The cover of nearby
gullies and creekbeds provide the permanent cover they need. Occasionally, you may walk a bird up in picked corn, but more often it will flush
wild or run back into cover. Some hunters who use flushing dogs walk
the easy route where field meets brush until their dogs pick up hot
scent, and then follow into the thick stuff. It seems to work.

permanent cover pheasants need, and often hold a bonus
covey of quail. The key is permanent cover. Unless there is
evidence that the cover has been there for several years—
evidence such as very high weeds, brushy tangles, young
trees, and so forth—you may as well not mess with it. But if
these indicators are present, you have to give the place a try.
It's your duty!

There are no hard and fast rules for how to hunt pheasant cover. It's just necessary to use your head. But here's
some general advice: keep quiet, work into the wind, cut off
escape routes, and approach each piece of cover as a tactical
maneuver in which the intended victims are as smart as you
are.

This hunter pushed a bird out of the last few yards of available cover.
When you work cover of any kind, make sure you walk through the last
few inches of it—that's where a rooster will be, if he's there at all.

By the way, I haven't mentioned the world famous and
critically acclaimed stop-and-go technique, so I will now.
Forget it. It's a waste of time because for one thing, the bird
may go from a place you don't want him to leave and/or
toward a place you'd just as soon he'd stay away from. I do
use the stop-and-go when my dog has a bird worked pretty
well but can't quite pin it, such as at the end of a brushy
draw when the bird won't allow himself to be pushed into
the air. Then, freezing the dog with a "Whoa" and pausing
myself, I can often make the nervous pheasant flush.

But as a general technique to flush birds that may or
may not be there, I don't use the stop-and-go. This tactic is
often suggested for the dogless hunter. I've got a different
tactic for that person: get a dog.

I don't mean to sound like a wise guy, but pheasants
take a lot of finding, a lot of killing, and a lot of catching if
they're crippled. I don't care if you were the anchorman on
your school's 440 team—you aren't going to outrun a
wingtipped rooster, not on your best day and his worst. To
the serious hunter, a dog is a great aid for finding birds in
the first place, pushing them into the air or pointing them,

Abandoned farmsteads near active crop fields are great pockets. Birds are reluctant to leave and will normally hold for dogs.

but the dog really comes into his own when he has to go after a downed bird.

Pheasants have to be hunted with the canniness and planning you'd associate with a military campaign. You can't stroll through the woods like you can with woodcock, depending entirely upon your dog's nose. You can't sit and wait, hidden, as you can in waterfowl hunting. You surely can't stand out in the open and take pops as birds swing by, as you can with doves. Fact is, you can't do anything except hunt the ringneck on his turf and on his terms. His relatives have been slickering your relatives for a few thousand years. He has a lot to lose compared to you. And he isn't afraid of you—he'll live in your wife's strawberry patch if you'll let him. He's just smart.

So you must analyze every piece of cover, be it field edge, brushy draw, slough, terrace, railroad right-of-way, or thicket, before you enter. You must go in with a plan, a plan that will cut off the pheasant's escape routes and put him in the air perplexed about where you came from and how you managed to do this. You and your dog must take his cover apart; you must not leave a blade of frost-withered grass unchecked, not a tuft unkicked.

You must push that cockbird from where he is to where you want him to be. You must push slowly and quietly so he doesn't take flight before you're ready and in range. You must push him to where his legs won't help him and he has to rely on his wings. Then you'll shoot pheasants.

IV
THE GUNS

I once met a man who told me that year in and year out he shot nine pheasants for every 10 shots. I found out later that he also collected Edsels. There has to be a connection there.

Let's sit down and freshen our glasses here, in this farmhouse that has been a half century of prairie winds. Let's smell the good smells coming from the kitchen and look out the dusty window panes at the rooster pheasants hung on the porch, their feathers glinting in the last light. And let's talk the good talk, you and I. Let's talk of the guns we'd like to own if our lives revolved totally around pheasants and pheasant hunting, and let's say—just for fun—that we could order up a gun that would do just what we wanted it to do when the dog finally cornered an old long-spurred cockbird right down there where the McInnis place meets the river.

The perfect pheasant gun hasn't been made—it won't be, either, because there isn't a perfect set of circumstances that we can factor into the equation. No two days are the same, and no two shots are ever identical. So like most things in life, a pheasant gun is a compromise.

I remember my first real pheasant hunt. I was 12, and the men around me were long of tooth when it came to understanding the bird. We met at a coffee shop and sorted out what we wanted to do and the places we wanted to hunt. This hunt was within the last couple of years of the Glory Days of pheasant abundance, and getting permission was no problem.

The dogs waited in the cars outside, and finally, after what seemed like hours, my companions swilled the last of their black coffee and we headed for the gunning grounds. Once the cars were parked, the gun cases came out, and out of the cases came long-barrelled, tightly choked pumps and autoloaders. The pumpgunners leaned toward the smooth of old Model 12 Winchester, while those with autos seemed to favor the Remington 11-48. Gauge was no question: they all shot 12s stuffed with high-brass No. 6 shot.

In those days, a half dozen men pushed big cornfields while a few others waited at the end for the inevitable explosion of birds, and the shooting was often at long range. So I guess the tight-shooting guns made sense.

Today, ranges are likely to be closer, and the hunter, perhaps a solitary figure plying the waste places, will be using a dog. Choosing a shotgun for today's pheasant gunning is more a matter of where and how you hunt. Let's take a look.

In England and on the Continent, pheasant shooting is just that—shooting. Driven birds, pen-raised until they are juveniles and then released on estates, are "presented" over the "guns" by drivers who push them into the air. At their appointed stations, the shooters stand fast and fire at incoming birds, some of which are high and all of which are fast. As a result, the pheasant shooter in that part of the world likely uses some sort of light "game gun," usually a 12 bore, but others, especially in France, prefer the 16. The loads are light for a couple of reasons: the shots are many and the guns are light, and if yon British gunner wishes to avoid being driven into the ground like a tent stake by recoil, he must use light loads. Secondly, the incoming bird has its vitals exposed to the shot charge, and when the incomer's speed collides with the outgoing shot charge, the collision is lethal.

Because an incoming bird must be led, such game guns are universally stocked high, to shoot about two feet high at 40 yards. Thus the shooter raises his gun, swings up through the bird, and touches off when the bead finds the target's head. Deadly.

In this country, we have an almost opposite situation. The birds are going away, but are still rising. The vitals are usually protected by heavy wings and heavier bone, and a solid charge of shot is needed to anchor a bird. However, I am of the persuasion that better shooting, rather than firepower, will bring more birds to hand.

Let's take the situation of using a flushing dog and see what our average pheasant hunter will need. The morning is snappy as the hunter releases his eager springer spaniel. After dashing off his edge a bit, the dog makes game in creekside cover or weed-infested fencerow. As the scent heats up, the dog moves ahead. The rooster legs it down the line and then bursts into the air. Unless the hunter is a near-relative of Jesse Owens, he will be at extreme range when the shot opportunity occurs—say, 35 yards. This calls for a gun with a fairly tight choke and big shot, something like a tight improved cylinder/modified or tight improved/full on a double, tight modified on a repeating gun.

At 35 yards, a rising pheasant takes more lead than you might think. True, he gets under way slowly, but so, really, does a shot charge. From the time a shooter's brain tells him to fire until the shot cloud gets downrange, a rooster

In this sequence, look for the amount of shot a rooster pheasant can take. The range is short, the load potent—a one-ounce load of No. 6 express, fired from a 20 gauge bored improved cylinder/modified. In the first frame, the young shooter, author's son Chris, flushes the bird ahead of a point by a setter, whose white color makes her hard to see here. The bird is rising, and Chris is starting to react . . .

The shot from the first barrel hits too far back. Feathers from the bird's rear section—that long, hypnotizing tail—are driven beyond the bird, which is still climbing. The shooter is doing a good job of keeping his face down and concentrating . . .

With feathers from the first hit still floating in the air, Chris fires his second, tighter barrel. Now the range has increased and the bird, at a slight angle, has vitals exposed to the shooter . . .

Hit by the second barrel, the bird falls. Both hits were necessary to drop this winter-tough rooster, although the bird would have been dead had he been hit farther forward with the first shot.

A hit far forward will normally result in a clean kill. This rooster was holding tight, a result of weather conditions that later brought on an ice storm. A high-shooting gun places the shot charge up front, in a pheasant's vitals . . .

can put some distance between himself and the ground. So a high-shooting gun is needed.

To get such a gun to shoot high—say, a foot high at 40 yards—it must be so stocked that you see, when your cheek is down, all of the barrel or rib, foreshortened greatly but visible if you look down at it. Another way is to take your empty gun and sight down it into a miror, pointing at your shooting eye in the reflection. The pupil of your shooting eye should be lined up a quarter inch above the rib; in other words, the bottom of the iris of your eye, the colored part, should be even with the top of the rib or barrel and the pupil above that.

If your gun is stocked thus, and a bird is rising, you can hold on him and knock him cold. Otherwise, you'll shoot into that mass of tailfeathers and cripple—and probably lose—the bird. A high-shooting gun also keeps your head down because you don't have to raise it to get a good look. True straightaways with no vertical lead required can be

. . . and often the bird is raked with shot from stem to stern. Note the feathers that have been loosened from the neck and head area, normally a sign of a clean kill. Also, the bird is dropping with his head starting to loll back, rather than erect and looking for escape once he hits the ground.

shot by holding slightly under the bird; give the target a seat on the end of your barrel and shoot.

If much of your shooting is over a pointing dog, as mine is, then again, a high-shooting gun is in order. Even though the time lapse between triggering and hit is shorter, the normally shorter ranges mean that the bird jumps relatively faster and angles are steeper.

But chokes should be more open. One of my pet wood-lot pheasant guns is also my pet grouse and woodcock gun. If that seems strange, let me elaborate. Over a pointing dog, the conditions of shooting pheasants, grouse, and woodcock have much in common: short ranges; close, quick shots;

An all-too-common sight among pheasant hunters: a going-away rooster dropping feathers from a hit too far back. Such hits often drive one or two shot into the vitals of a bird, causing death later on. Unlike doves, quail, grouse, woodcock, and other upland birds, pheasants that are body-shot often don't end up in the hunter's bag. The pheasant shooter must concentrate on the forward parts of his target—and that white ring is a natural pointing area.

rising targets. I shoot this piece because the chokes are open—improved cylinder/modified—and the gun has two triggers, so I can select the chokes almost instantly. This gun is, I should tell you, a five-pound, 14-ounce Parker 16 gauge, a bore that has fallen from popularity. But I find that over pointing dogs, the 2½-dram, one-ounce loading of No. 6 shot is deadly on close-flushing pheasants. The high-shooting stock places the pattern in the head and neck of a rising bird, and very few birds do not hit the ground dead if I do my part. Over dogs, and at ranges of 15-25 yards, there's no need for Roman-candle shells and deck-gun borings; save those for the end of a western cornfield.

By the way, this game gun, when loaded with a pow-derpuff, one-ounce load of No. 8s, has done well in the grouse and woodcock thickets of a dozen states and Canadian provinces. The gun's weight, that of a light 20 bore, makes it easy to carry, yet nothing patterns an ounce of shot as well as a 16.

A gun's fit and balance will go a long way toward making you a better pheasant shot. Most guns don't come right off the store rack with a comb high enough for me. Since I like shooting *up* at a bird and having the built-in vertical lead I talked about, and since I want to get my eye a quarter inch above the rib, I've tried a variety of ways to get this done.

You can buy some common stick-on moleskin from the drugstore and build up the stock in layers until you have the proper sight picture. Or you could build the comb up with self-hardening resin or even plastic wood—I've done both. But the best way is to have a new stock mode in the proper dimensions, determined by one of the methods I've talked about.

Now, a new stock isn't cheap, but it sure beats missing or crippling all the time, so consider it. Barring that, you could invest in stock bending. Some firms do this, and most gunsmiths can put you in touch with a stock bender. Essentially, the grip area of the stock is heated with hot oil, which softens the wood. Then, in a bending jig, the stock is canted upward until the comb (where your face goes) and the heel (top of the stock in the rear) are at the right elevation. If the bend is severe, the stock man will sometimes have to recut the angle of the butt because the pitch will have been changed, but that's small potatoes. A bent stock is cheaper than a new one and in many ways is preferable because the factory inletting and wood-to-metal fit are unaffected. Same wood—different shape.

Occasionally, you'll have to work the comb *down* to get the right picture, especially if you're shooting a European gun and you're a little round in the face. Then, coarse sandpaper—a little rubbing at a time with a lot of testing—

will do the trick. After the proper level is reached, use progressively finer grades of paper, ending with the finest grit you can get so that the wood is merely polished.

Then refinish the whole stock with a good stock finish. There are many, but my taste runs to a coat of spar varnish first, which I allow to dry completely and then sand down to the bare wood—which fills the pores of the wood. Then I rub in linseed oil or Linspeed Oil. After each coat dries, buff it down with 000 steel wool for a nice gloss. About five coats will protect as much as 500, so you don't have to overdo it.

A good-fitting gun helps, but so does a well-balanced one. The definition of balance is ambiguous at best. So much depends upon personal taste, and what the shooter is used to, that it's tough to tackle the subject.

To be well balanced, a shotgun's weight should be equally held between the two hands, and the concentration of the weight should be at or near a point about four inches ahead of the trigger—at the hinge pin or "knuckle" of a double.

For some purposes, say on guns meant for pass-shooting waterfowl or doves, the weight should be a bit farther forward. A weight-forward gun allows for a smooth swing with less hitching and stopping of the swing. If the weight is forward but is nominal—in other words, if the gun is not too heavy—you've got a sweet-swinging piece. You've probably read and heard many times that a heavy gun is harder to stop, making for a smooth swing; well, a heavy gun is also harder to *start*, sometimes making for *no* swing in tight cover.

Inversely, the barrel-light gun has certain advantages. The 16 gauge I mention in this chapter is distinctly muzzle-light, with the balance point located a full inch to the rear of the knuckle. This gun is used for fast points at twisting, jinking targets in thick, early-season cover. As a pheasant gun, it's limited to snap shooting in close quarters, such as thickets and brushy woodlots.

Ideally, the weight-between-the-hands gun will start

This pheasant hunter—of the generation that remembers well the post-war Glory Days—still clings to his Model 12, the gun often called the "perfect repeater." Plugged to hold only three shells to conform to law, 12-gauge pump guns of various models have probably accounted for more pheasants than all other actions combined. Lighter and better-balanced than autoloaders, and thoroughly reliable, pumps are probably still the No. 1 choice.

quickly and swing smoothly. If it does not, you can lighten the stock, or weight it by adding lead to the hole behind the recoil pad. If barrels are too long, you might consider having them bobbed and installing screw-in chokes. On a double, 26 inches seems right, and the same holds for repeaters, although the repeater's overall length will be three or four inches more than the double's.

Gun weight depends on what you consider to be heavy. I see no reason for a pheasant gun to weigh more than 7½ pounds or less than six—beyond these extremes, you get into trouble.

Barrel length is a matter of preference. If shots are

long, longer barrels up to 28 inches give a smoother swing. But in close, 26-inch tubes do well. In a repeater, a gun with a 26-inch barrel and screw-in chokes is invaluable, and a 26-inch barrel bored modified or tight improved cylinder is fine.

So here it is, the ideal—six to 7½ pounds, straight stock that shoots a tad high, weight equally balanced around the receiver with neither a barrel nor a stock bias, 26 to 28-inch barrel or barrels, and the choke depending upon the conditions where you hunt.

My son Chris has the reflexes of a teenager—which he is—and does very well on dog-pointed pheasants with a little 20 side-by-side choked improved/modified. With its 25-inch barrels, his pheasant gun is very quick in the thick stuff, which is where I send him while I stay outside and wait for the easy shots; usually, there aren't any shots for me, just one crisp crack to mark his location, followed by his familiar cackle of glee.

A couple of seasons ago, we were hunting woodcock when we came to a thick growth of red-osier dogwood bordering a picked cornfield. He had his 20, I my Parker, and we'd seen few woodcock, most of them having flighted through previously. But in that dogwood were a half dozen rooster pheasants that had been driven from the field by the combine which had knocked over the corn. We switched from No. 8s to 6s and took our limits of roosters with those same guns. My setter gave us marvelous points, and the shots were short and through brush or not taken at all. Like so many of today's pheasant-hunting situations, the birds were in the hard-to-reach places, more like typical grouse and woodcock cover. So Chris and I used what we had, grouse and woodcock guns, and did well.

As long as I'm on the subject, you've probably figured out that I think the side-by-side double is probably the best pheasant gun for most shooting conditions. It permits very accurate vertical pointing, more so than a single-sighting-plane gun such as an over/under or repeater. For birds that are normally rising, the side-by-side is best; for crossing

The Remington 870 may be *the* most popular slide action of all time in terms of numbers sold. Most experts agree that a 16, 20, and even a 28 gauge on occasion will kill pheasants. But for all shooting, day in and day out, the 12 gauge is the best choice. (Photo by Joe Workosky)

targets, the single plane is better. The live-pigeon shooters of the world, at least many of them, go with the side-by-side double for this very reason, and they are often shooting for huge prizes and side bets.

One advantage of doubles is that you can have different boring and carry different loads in each barrel—with screw-in choke tubes, the options are almost numerous enough to drive you crazy. You can carry a high-base No. 6 in the right barrel and a high-base No. 5 or No. 4 in the left, and have great range coverage.

But the shooter of a repeating gun can do the same. Here's one way: load the chamber with a No. 6 high brass, the first shell in the magazine (the third shot fired) with a No. 4, and the last shell another No. 6 or a No. 5. If you can stand the accounting and have enough pockets, it's a dream. Bird goes up—*wham!* (No. 6), you miss . . . *wham!* (No. 5) . . . he's still going . . . *wham!* (No. 4). By working with your gun and observing patterns, you can work in loads that will give you a pheasant-killing pattern at 25, 35, and 45 yards by varying the load. If you do it right, the patterns will look nearly the same—the 25-yard pattern with one load looking a lot like the 45-yard sheet with another load.

Since it's important that you be aware of *where* you shoot, pattern testing and stock fitting go together. The English method of shooting at washed plates as fast as you can comfortably and smoothly mount and shoot is a good one. You may find that your gun isn't throwing the shot where you'd like. Once you've established this, a barrel man or stockmaker can usually make the needed adjustments: stocks can be sanded, bent, and cast off or cast on; barrels can be regulated at the muzzle and, with a pump or auto, bent so that the shot is hitting where you want it to.

Also, having a good idea of what the shot spread looks like on paper gives you more confidence and improves your judgment about what shots are "hittable" and what ones aren't.

When patterning, I'd suggest you shoot at distances of 10, 20, 30, and finally 40 yards—and maybe even at 45 yards. That way, you get an idea of how your gun and load are performing at a variety of ranges.

I once had a nice little 20 gauge with three-inch chambers that I used on pheasants occasionally. The 40-yard patterns were great with No. 6 shot, one-ounce loads. But I had a hard time with the right—modified—barrel at shots 15 to 18 yards out. I finally patterned it at that range and found that the shot was clumping for some reason; the gun shot extra-full close in, even tighter than the properly shooting left barrel, which *was* bored full. A gunsmith opened the right barrel about six-thousandths, and all was fine.

A hit too far off center. This bird is dropping due to a broken left wing, which means it will hit the ground running. Shooters should try to "read" a hit so that they know what is likely to happen after the shot. In thick cover, with the bird's legs intact, chances of recovery are slim without a very good dog. If a bird rolls to one side after the shot, it usually indicates a broken wing; a dropped leg usually means a shot up into the body cavity and a dead bird right where he comes down.

If you shoot your patterns correctly—point and shoot without aiming—you'll get an idea of how the gun is shooting for you. There is no way to make the proper adjustments to comb, heel, and pitch of the stock without shooting patterns. If your patterns seem to be centering a bit low, even though they are otherwise acceptable in terms of density, you need a straighter stock. Normally, having the gun impact its load a half-pattern high is right; in other words, the point of aim should be covered by the bottom third of the shot spread.

For many hunters, the 20 gauge fills the need for a

light gun with short barrels and a lively feel—my definition of a good pheasant gun. In side-by-side or over/under configuration, most 20s these days can handle 2¾-inch and three-inch magnum shells if you feel you need them, but the one-ounce load is normally sufficient for today's pheasants, shot placement being the more important killing factor. But still, I'd have at least one barrel choked full and a short magnum load of 1⅛ ounces of No. 6 in that barrel. Because the 20 gauge (and the 16 in case you're a throwback like me) with its smaller bore has less pattern efficiency than a 12 gauge, you'll get more stringing of shot, so you'll need to tighten down the choke.

Pheasants have to be hit hard, and they have to be hit in the vitals. I've found it usually takes at least four pellets in No. 6 size or larger in the vitals to anchor a rooster, and you have to break bone. Unlike some other, more fragile birds, ringnecks take a lot of punch.

Day in and day out, No. 6 is probably the best choice, and I want at least an ounce of it. In a 12 gauge, you've got options the other gauges don't allow. However, shotgun shooting nowadays is more a function of shot load and choke than it is of gauge. If you are going to shoot an ounce of shot, you should have a tighter choke than if you were shooting 1⅛ or 1¼ ounces.

One late season, my son had excellent luck shooting his 20 double (a new gun with chrome-lined barrels) at pheasants with one ounce of *steel* 6s at wide-flushing birds. The steel shot was in a three-inch magnum shell, and it belted him pretty good, but he fired only four times to kill his limit of three birds, so it wasn't too bad.

I've used steel No. 4s (which approximate lead No. 6) while hunting pheasants in a waterfowl management area in Nebraska where lead shot was not allowed. The steel shot practically eliminates the need for forward allowance when shots are within 15 yards, as over a dog. And the steel patterns tighter because it isn't mashed flat like soft lead shot as it passes through the bores. A steel shot, being lighter than a lead shot of equal size, starts off quite a bit faster. It shows down faster, too, and duck hunters have had to learn to lead birds less when they're in close, and more than they're well out there, than they would with lead shot.

I know fellows who shoot *only* steel 6s at pheasants. By the way, if your gun is fairly new and in sound condition, steel won't affect the bores. A lot of that hoopla about steel shot reaming out shotgun bores came early on and was more an advertising ploy than anything. I've shot steel for years at ducks through a beautiful, 40-year-old Model 12, and I've never seen a hint of damage.

Here's a piece of Americana for you. One gun I've enjoyed on pheasants is a 16 gauge hammer gun that was given to me by noted author Gene Hill. Now, a hammer gun these days is a rarity. The truth is, the day of the shotguns with outside hammers was a fleeting one, especially those with fluid steel—non-Damascus—barrels. So quickly did the hammerless guns come along that the period when the fluid steel, exposed-hammer shotgun held sway was only about 15 years.

Still, there is something to be said for them. They are fun guns, and they offer a subliminal urge to get your face down on the stock where it belongs. The hammers, visible peripherally, from a square with a mark in the middle, above the barrels and between the hammers.

Hunting with one of these guns is not as difficult as you might think. There is no safety, so the hammers are carried at the half-cock position. When the dog starts making game or a pointing dog locks up, you just cock the hammers and walk in.

But as often as not, you'll be hunting with a flushing dog or with a pointing breed that's having a tough time holding running birds, so if you ever get the chance to pick up an old but solid hammer gun and would like to hunt with it, and you're concerned about getting it into action fast, here's what I do: I load the gun, cock it, but don't close it. When a pheasant jumps, I just close the gun and am ready for action. In reality, the closing of such a piece takes no more time than pushing a safety forward or sideways. And you always have a little time lag with pheasants because you must identify the bird as a rooster and not a hen before you start shooting.

A hammer gun carried in this manner is incredibly safe, much safer than a conventional, modern double carried closed with the safety on. And with almost no practice at all, you'll learn to close the gun and be on the mark as quickly as with any other shotgun.

I've used this technique on pheasants many times, and even on birds as fast as ruffed grouse and woodcock, and have had few problems—my misses were due not to speed but to lousy shooting.

Shooting a pheasant is not a very tough proposition in most cases, not compared with shooting ruffed grouse, woodcock, or quail in thick cover; certainly the shooting itself is nothing compared with the difficulty of getting a shot in the first place.

The act of hitting a pheasant with a high-shooting gun encompasses almost every facet of wingshooting. In the thickets of the East, the fast swing that grouse hunters use is effective. In the West, if it's your turn at the end of a cover patch, a smooth, sustained-lead swing is better. A pheasant just getting under power ahead of a dog should be duck soup if you keep your wits; a downwind ringneck with a boiler of steam up is another matter.

Once, in Nebraska, I stood at the corner of a cornfield and shot at roosters the drivers were pushing past me. The birds were 30-40 yards out and just skimming the corn, the wind at their backs. I shot at four without cutting a feather, getting more frustrated all the time. Finally, in anger, I sarcastically doubled my lead and killed the next one stone dead. The same with the next. It's amazing how far you have to lead a rooster in full flight.

In the terraced farm fields of Iowa, my dog and I, hunting alone, were surrounded by roosters. We'd pushed them along a terrace to where it narrowed near a hill. The birds

A pair of lucky hunters and unlucky young birds caught in open stubble at first light. In the Glory Days, the philosophy was: "If it ain't a full-chocked 12, it ain't a gun." On the left, a humpbacked Browning Auto-5; on the right, a Model 12 Winchester, its bluing only a memory. (MI DNR photo)

were bunched, and the little dog, poor thing, was permanently locked into a walking point.

Finally the birds started coming up in twos and singles. I was using a little six-pound 12 gauge with 25-inch barrels bored tight improved cylinder and full, and I started shooting. I dropped three birds by doubling on the first rise, winging a big bird with the first barrel after reloading, and then shooting that same bird again in the upper body as it dropped. If I can see life in a cockbird as it drops, I drive another shot into it immediately while I have the chance. My dog appreciates finding and fetching dead roosters, although she loves a good scrap with a cripple once in a while.

Anyway, these birds were like tin cans on a fence post. They rose straight up, and the high-shooting gun took them easily. There was no apparent lead, only the placement of the gun's pattern a half pattern above the point of aim. That's all the lead that was necessary. Even *I* could hit them.

The point is, if you can get a pheasant to fly under your terms, the shooting is normally easier. If he flies at his choice, the shots will be long or fast or both. Good hunting methods simplify shooting.

A rooster pheasant is over one-third tail, and that tail makes you want to shoot at the middle of the bird. Ruffed grouse and woodcock hunters, along with quail shooters, are used to shooting at the *bird*; the pheasant hunter has to think in terms of the *head*. I've found that in order to kill a rooster pheasant stone dead so that I can meander over and pick him up, I have to break a wing, or a leg, and put shot into the vitals. Friend, if you don't do that, you won't get him. He's tough; in his own way, he is as tough as a wild turkey. I mean, even when you clean a wild rooster, you have to have a *sharp* knife. A hand axe works better than anything for taking off the wings and the head, he's that tough.

A friend and I were whiling away an afternoon with some early-season pheasants at a shooting preserve, basically getting our dogs in shape. He commented on how it seems that No. 7½ shot was all he really needed for pheasants, and then he added: ". . . for *preserve* pheasants." We both know that these birds, pen reared, just do not possess the physical toughness—the hardness of bone and tissue— that wild birds have. Sure, a dense cloud of an ounce or 1⅛ ounces of 7½s make a dandy load, but for the wild birds of

Dave Meisner, Iowa native and expert pheasant hunter, does his early gunning with an over/under 20 gauge and one-ounce No. 6 loads. If quail are around, always a plains-state possibility, he switches to No. 7½. (Dave Meisner photo)

November, they lack the bone-breaking, tissue-splitting strength that roosters have to be hit with.

The method that works the best is driving shot into the front portions of a bird. A rooster coming off the ground, for most people, is a gorgeous sight: it stirs the senses, and it excites the mind. It makes the glands open and secrete their chemical messengers into the blood. These hormones do strange things to bird hunters—they give them pheasant fever.

In its advanced form, pheasant fever makes the victim

snatch off a shot which hits the bird too far back; anything behind the wing joints is too far back. The bird falls with its head up. When you see a mature pheasant dropping from the November sky this way, you can be sure you and your dog are going to have a job on your hands, because this pheasant is going to be difficult to bring to possession.

Try to remember that a pheasant can be deceptively fast, even when rising. If he has the wind behind him, he's even faster. A going-away rooster presents some of birdom's hardest bone and gristle to the shooter, bone that is tough to break and gristle that's tough to penetrate. So it is essential that you try to see the bird's eye, his white ring, the engorged face, and think of *that* as your target. If you do, the pattern will be placed where it belongs, up front, and your birds will start hitting the ground dead instead of running.

A fast swing is a good method of pheasant shooting, with the gun being rapidly mounted as the body and hands are pivoting to overtake the mark. By the time gunstock reaches your face, the lead is pretty well established. This is a simplified version of the English Churchill method, and it works. You must *see* the bird. You must *concentrate* on the head and neck. The gun must flow to the face as your body pivots to follow the bird. The forward allowance, or lead, is all about taken care of if you do these things. You should, as much as possible, be unaware of the barrels, much like a pane of glass you are looking through. Sure, the barrel is there, but don't look *at* it, look *past* it.

You'll get more up-front hits if you wait to clearly see a passing rooster, because once you start after him, you will be doing a lot of catching up, and this is where the speed of swing will get you up toward the front of the bird. A slow swing is what often cripples pheasants, so I'd suggest that you make every effort to trigger the shot as the butt of the gun touches your shoulder. The English go so far as to teach a method whereby the trigger has finger pressure on it as the butt heads toward the shoulder, so that the force of the gun hitting your shoulder pocket, completing the gun mount, fires the shot. It works.

A good shooting percentage on pheasants is fairly easy. Over a dog, where the birds are coming up in good range, there's no reason not to hit three out of four, although reportedly the national average is one in three.

Killing a pheasant in the air is tough, but merely dropping one is not, so if the bird drops with his head up, be ready to drive shot into him again while you have the chance, or you'll be sorry you didn't. If the bird drops with his head lolled back across his breast or back, you should still hurry over, but you'll probably be all right.

Once, in Nebraska, I put my father on the end of a fence row and circled a quarter mile to drive the cover toward him. He's a good shot with years of experience and owns a Model 12 that fits him like a glove, and he stood there and dropped his limit of four roosters with that many shots, bouncing them into the plowed field that bordered the cover. Each bird had been shot well up front; shattered beaks and bloodied necks showed where his high-base 5s had driven into the vitals. Later, on that same trip, I got a simultaneous rise of three cocks and shot all three with my 12 gauge autoloader. They were all rising and heading away, and I picked them all off. My golden retriever found but one, and that one only barely. The lesson continues— shoot up front.

If you can get yourself to lead roosters far enough, crossing shots are the most deadly of the readily available shots because more of the vital organs are exposed to the shot string. In South Dakota, my son and I flushed a low, going-away bird my dog had been working. The bird came off the ground at 15 yards, and we were both on him right away. Chris hit him solidly with his 20, a one-ounce load of 6s; I hit the bird with my 12, 1¼ ounces of 6s, and the boy also fired his left barrel. The dog pinned the bird down 25 yards from us—still alive and blinking at us. The feathers in the grass could have stuffed a small pillow. The next bird was a short crosser that Chris grassed at 20 yards as dead as a box of rocks—but this tme the chance to hit the vitals had been there.

An inexpensive field stock can be worked up with epoxy or wood filler to raise the comb, thus making for a high-shooting piece. Expensive, figured stocks should be bent by a competent stockmaker.

Fast gun handling is usually a function of cover, and in much of the pheasant's range in the eastern part of the United States, that means the brushy woodlots of farm country. Often these areas are all the habitat that is available to the birds, so they use them for cover and shelter. In there they behave like grouse, and sometimes you have to be unbelievably quick to take the birds.

In Michigan's Thumb, once storied pheasant country, Chuck Lichon and I were hunting a couple of falls ago. The farm we were hunting reminded me of farms 20 years ago—a little on the "dirty" side with wide fencerows and some fallow fields. But the birds were in the woodlots and were running. Charlie worked his Lab, Jill, through the cover while I blocked, looking ·for a shot. But the birds stayed in, circling and circling, until finally I came in to help. The extra set of feet started putting birds into the air, and we got action.

The point is, the pheasants weren't anxious to get up, so shots were close and very grouse-like, with the birds coming up through openings and heading for holes in the canopy. In areas where we seek eastern farm-country ring-necks, we're also likely to find flighting and native woodcock—the terrain has the same density of stems, understory, and moist conditions. The woodcock are there because of the moisture and the cover; the pheasants are there for the cover, which is a function of that moisture. Anyway, in such cover, a pheasant looks anything but slow.

V
THE PLACES

The best place to hunt pheasants is a place that has pheasants. If that sounds simple, it's because it is. Notice that I didn't say a thing about "easy."

Although we often think of the pheasant as an import, he's a bird that has been welcomed wherever he has set up housekeeping. Let's take a look at some of those places.

In England, where pheasants have thrived for hundreds of years, the ringneck has been gunned from the time of top-hatted, landed gentry with flintlocks up until today, when many large estates have been turned over to "syndicates" that sell the shooting rights on a day-to-day basis. Travel outfits bring in foreign shooters to experience the driven-pheasant shoots as they existed in the days of Edward VII.

If you want to experience a driven shoot on an estate, there are agencies in America that can book you into one and also arrange side excursions. These estates are managed by a gamekeeper, a "moleskin" in the vernacular—a reflection of his clothing, once made from the skins of moles he'd caught. The gamekeeper's job is to rear pheasants, release them so that they can strengthen their flight muscles, and then arrange drives with beaters, the drives moving pheasants out of cover and over the heads of a line of shooters ("guns") so as to present the most difficult shooting. A high pheasant ("tall" or an "Archangel"—don't you love the way the British talk?) that's clipping along with a tailwind is a tough target, so difficult that taking one bird with four shells is considered good shooting.

There's an old saying among pheasant hunters: "Never ask permission to hunt any farm next to a blacktop road." These late-season hunters got the green light to work a honey-hole of congregated roosters well off the beaten path and bagged a few. Late-season permission is often easier to gain because crops have been taken off by then. If you ask, the landowner may even join you.

In England, Scotland, Wales, and Ireland, such shoots begin on October 1 and normally end on or about the first of February. The drive itself is an interesting exercise in logistics.

On the day of the shoot, the gamekeeper assembles a number of the locals who, apparently, have nothing better to do. These people are placed in a line next to a strip of cover, normally a woodlot. The guns are lined up at shooting positions chosen by lot. These positions will rotate on progressive drives so that each gun has an equal chance at birds.

At a signal, the beaters move into the cover, tapping trees with sticks and kicking tufts of grass with their feet. They move slowly and relatively silently, because if there were a Cemetary Ridge-type charge, the birds would depart *en masse* and the shooting would be at one huge flock in which few birds would be downed. Instead, the birds come over in pairs and threes and fours, offering sustained shooting throughout the drive.

The only talking among the beaters is the expession "cock up," which means to be alert because of the flush of a woodcock, the European version of our own, a larger bird but still a difficult target.

In the old days, the guns would take nearly everything that was driven out of the cover—pheasants, snipe, woodcock, rabbits, hares, and probably hedgehogs if they had the chance. On the syndicate shoots, it is often requested that the guns take only the pheasants. Remember, a British request carries some weight; I think Tennyson's storied cavalry unit of 600 was "requested" to charge the Russian artillery in the Crimean War.

The guns, for their part, must be safe and sportsmanlike—no poaching your neighbor's birds, no firing down toward the beaters, and no low shots. The birds that come over, then, are typically high incomers with perhaps slight angles.

A little more about guns. High-shooting guns, ones which will give the required built-in lead without covering the bird, are preferred. I have a French gun, built for the European 2½-inch shell ("cartridge") and having 27½-inch barrels. It is very light for a 12 bore, weighing but five pounds, 10 ounces, and looking down the rib is like looking down a long hill—or maybe *up* would explain it better. This gun places its patterns a full two feet high at 40 yards, meaning the center of the shot grouping is out of the traditional 30-inch patterning circle at that range.

With such a gun, you can point at the head of a driven bird and thereby automatically add two feet of lead. These guns are really of no use for anything else.

In England, the "Best" gun is built for pheasant shooting by such firms as Purdey, Holland & Holland, W & C Scott, Powell, and a host of others. These guns, made entirely by hand, are said to have the ability to withstand years of the punishing pounding that goes with driven-bird shooting. Not too long ago, a dedicated shooter with sufficient time and money would expect to fire 10,000 shots a year from his two or three Best guns. Today, not nearly that number is fired, and on the syndicate shoots, one gun that you load yourself is the rule.

Much of the reputation that London and Birmingham Best guns have for durability can be traced to a couple of things. First, the shells fired—and 12 bore is the most popular by nearly a 10-to-one margin—are the little 1¹⁄₁₆-ounce British field loads 2½ inches in length. They do not generate the huge force of recoil that the maximum-load, 1¼-ounce shell we shoot here does. Secondly, it has long been the custom of users of Best guns to send them back to the maker each year to have the locks cleaned, the gun inspected, and perhaps the finish touched up.

The maker, then, is free to replace any parts that show wear and to tighten the action. Friends, if you shot powderpuffs through your Winchester and sent it back to the factory every year, your gun would last forever, too. Thus, almost any shotgun made with modern steels and manufacturing methods is a durable gun.

I was at a Sporting Clays shoot in Houston a couple of

years ago, and quite a number of the Texans were carrying London Best guns. I commented on my durability theory— not meaning to take anything away from the remarkable reliability of a Purdey or a Boss or any other maker. One Texan said that was fine, but he'd never sent his gun back to the manufacturer and he'd been shooting it for 10 years. I asked how much he shot it, and he figured about four or five boxes of shells a year. Hmmmm.

A lot of shooters would be more likely to put at least that number of shells through a pump gun or auto in a single day's practice on clay birds—plus a lot more on various kinds of game in a year's time. Why doesn't this man use his gun that much? There's a reason, of course, and that reason is price. Nigel Beaumont, a friend of mine, is one of the Directors of James Purdey & Sons of Audley Street in London. On one of his visits to this country, we talked about the prices of the Purdey Best Gun—that firm's only grade. At the time, it took three years and cost 25,000 Yankee bucks to get one. Since that time, the dollar has strengthened against the British pound, but even now, $20,000 has to be considered the norm. A fellow does not take that kind of gun into a duck blind and fire high-brass 5s through it all day. He shoots light loads and sends it in every year or two to get it tuned up—I would, anyway.

Anyhow, back to the drive. The birds are up and coming over. The guns are firing, and birds are dropping. Labrador retrievers and their handlers stand ready to go after runners and cripples, the dead birds being left where they are until the drive is over. In England, game is a crop to be sold at market. Each gun is given the traditional brace or two of birds, but the rest go to defray some of the enormous costs of rearing birds and maintaining the land.

Regardless of what you may have read or heard, it is considered bad form to keep track of how many birds you shoot, although humans being what they are, I'm sure everybody does it. It is bad form, also, to shoot a repeating gun—it's doubles only, with the over/under gaining acceptance. Strangely, it seems that many Britons are using Japanese guns or those of Spanish origin built on the game-gun design: straight grip, splinter fore-end, weight around 6½ pounds in 12 gauge—preferring, I guess, to save their money for the shooting. The Spanish firm of AYA does a fine business in Britain, as does Winchester with its 101 over/under.

After the drive, the gamekeeper will move the guns to another location where another drive will take place. Usually, a lunch is provided at this time. In the evening a formal dinner is held at the manor house.

The gamekeeper, the evening or early morning before each shoot, will walk the edges of the property, flushing any straying birds back toward the center of the estate and shooting any that flush and are flying off the property. Sometimes visiting guns are taken along on such "rough" shoots to take care of those birds not cooperating.

Such a shoot is expensive, easily running into the low to mid four figures, but it's bound to be a lifetime memory. While you're there, take time to visit some of the gun rooms or maybe arrange for a shoot with a British coach at a shooting school. They can teach you a lot.

Today shoots in the British manner are being offered in Denmark and Hungary, and despite the expense, Americans flock to them. The pheasant as a "blueblood," however, is really no different from the bird that fools our dogs and laughs at us here in the States. Only the pomp and ceremony change.

East of the Mississippi, pheasant shooting is, for now, an iffy proposition. There are birds, but right now they are scattered and wary. Since pheasants do not do well in unglaciated, lime-free soils, the South is largely eliminated as pheasant range, so the Great Lakes states and the New England area are about it in the East.

Many of us were weaned on pheasants. As a kid, I experienced bird numbers in Michigan equal to about what eastern Iowa boasts today. That's probably true of many states, including the once-great pheasant state of Pennsylvania.

Sometimes you hit it right. Roosters tend to gather together late in the season; if you find one, you may find more. During a late hunt, three shooters took their combined limit of nine birds in a morning. Note that all three guns are straight-gripped (English), straight-stocked models— two 20 gauges and a light 12.

In the East, the hunting is a rough affair. Sloughs, swamps, waste patches, and unspeakable thickets are where pheasants hang out, and it is there you have to go to get them. Each bird is a trophy, though, perhaps tougher to bring to bag than a whitetail buck in the same locale. The proof? In Pennsylvania, they shoot almost twice as many deer as they do pheasants. It's similar in other eastern states that have seasons on both.

Over the next decade, a lot of that may well change as embattled farmers take advantage of the Farm Bill's Conservation Reserve provisions and start setting land aside and out of crop production. This is going to give the birds the habitat—particularly for nesting and for wintering-over—

that they're going to need, and the populations should start bouncing back.

In the East, my experience has been that standing water is a good bet for pheasants. In such places—cattail sloughs and the like that the farmer hasn't gotten around to draining yet—the vegetation is normally permanent. If cropland is nearby, this is going to be your best bet.

In the Midwest—the Plains States—the ringneck starts to show his stuff. The greater amount of habitat and the farming of grains that are ideal ringneck food—especially corn—give the pheasant a nice place to live.

For years South Dakota was the pheasant capital, and it still holds its share of birds. But much of that state's success was due to the Soil Bank program, which is now defunct. Let's hope that the Farm Bill does what observers hope it will do and replaces that program effectively. If so, it may prove to be the single most important boon to domestic wildlife in the last 30 years.

Nebraska is another place where pheasants are king, and the numbers should start coming up there as well. The central section is better than the eastern part of the state, I think, simply because farms are bigger and the amount of waste space on each is greater. The state regularly harvests a million birds and draws hunters from all over the country.

Iowa has led the nation in pheasant kill much of the last decade. Part of that success has to do with the high population, naturally, but another part is a matter of accessibility—Iowa's a whole lot closer to the metro centers of the East than South Dakota, Nebraska, or Kansas. The Iowa season traditionally starts the first Saturday of November and runs through the first Saturday of January or thereabouts, but early winters normally shut things off about the middle of December—you just can't get into the fields after that.

Kansas, on the other hand, offers shooting right through the end of January. Being a bit farther south than Iowa, its winter weather is not quite as severe, and the populations of birds and hunters are still high after Christmas. For a long time a sleeper as a pheasant state, Kansas has been recognized for what it is and is now attracting its share of out-of-staters.

Farther west, Montana, Wyoming, Idaho, Washington, Oregon—where all this foolishness got started—and California hold good numbers of birds. In the West, big-game hunting is king. I know many folks out there who won't bend a primer on anything smaller than a two-month meat supply. The result is that the birds in many places take a back seat to antelope, mule deer, and elk.

For example, in Wyoming you can hunt pheasants, chukars, Hungarian partridge, sharptails, prairie chickens, ruffed grouse, and sage hens without having to do very much driving around. But the problem here is one of distance from home. The local hunters are big-game oriented; out-of-staters find it difficult and time-consuming to get there, and the result is that the bird hunting often goes begging.

Heading for Iowa from Michigan last year, I saw license plates from all over the East, and the dog crates in the vehicles told me these folks were heading for the storied shooting grounds of the Midwest and West to hunt pheasants—that plus I asked a lot of people at gas stations and restaurants. I saw people from as far off as Vermont who were heading for South Dakota for the pheasant hunting. For many, such trips are a yearly event.

But many people botch up such a trip because of poor planning. There is no reason to, though. In all of the major pheasant states, the bird is a lure to bring in those out-of-state dollars. Thus game departments are more than willing to provide you with all you need to know in order to give it a try. So your first contact should be with the game department's division of public relations—normally called I & E for Information and Education. Make a call or write and tell them that you're planning a trip and ask for as much information as they have about the pheasant shooting.

Presently you'll receive in the mail a package containing enough stuff to get you drooling: maps, license applica-

A good chance from the good old days—the era of the Soil Bank program. These hunters worked fallow, set-aside acreage. (MI DNR photo)

tions, listings of motels and campgrounds, folders and flyers telling you the best places and methods to try, and advice on when to come. These media kits are not just fluff—they contain some good information because the folks there want you to come and enjoy yourself. That way, you and your dollars will come back.

Your next step is to start writing letters or making phone calls to line up accommodations, either at motels that take dogs (most in pheasant country do) or at campgrounds. I've done both, and I much prefer the motel route, but that's personal preference. If you have equipment like a travel trailer for lodging, you're nuts not to use it.

Before making the final commitment about where you're going to stay, determine *when* you want to go. It's no secret that opening day is the best time to hunt pheasants. But in most of the pheasant states of the Midwest and West, opening day is like a national holiday. Friends and relatives show up at farms, and the locals sometimes turn out in droves. If you have a place where you're guaranteed hunting, then go on the opener. Otherwise, I'd wait for a while.

Opening day finds a lot of cover and a lot of birds, birds which are relatively stupid—or at least as stupid as pheasants ever get. The young birds are experiencing their first-ever time under the guns, and they provide great sport for the first hours of the first day.

But the birds wise up fast, and then that huge amount of cover becomes a problem. Many states try to set the opener late enough so that crops—especially corn—are off, but it doesn't always work out that way. In 1985, two weeks of rain hit the corn belt, and when I headed for Iowa for the first day, my contacts ahead told me that the corn was still up. It should have been down, but it wasn't. Well, the birds were slippery after the first day, and the standing corn made things worse.

After opening day, pheasant hunting becomes a series of tradeoffs. If you wait until later in the season to go, you trade lower numbers of birds for smaller patches of cover; you trade skittish, wary pheasants for easier hunting conditions (barring snow); and you trade fewer opportunities for less competition.

I've always felt that unless I can make it on opening day with a guaranteed place to hunt, I'll wait at least two weeks before I go out. The third weekend of the season is a good time. Many out-of-state hunters and almost all of the resident hunters have been in the field and had some shooting, and the edge is off. The out-of-staters have gone home, and many local hunters don't have the same urge they did just a couple weeks before.

Also, many residents are waiting for Thanksgiving, when friends and relatives wend their way back home for a traditional shoot. When I was in college, a pal and I drove all night to get to Iowa for a quick hunt over our Thanksgiving break. It was a disaster because we couldn't get on any place—all the landowners were saving the birds for the folks who were either there or on their way.

So, with the seasons in most major pheasant states opening around the first part of November, I can't be more specific about when to go. If you don't have a good setup for opening day, wait until after Thanksgiving.

Late in the season, the cover diminishes faster than do the birds. Later—after the season closes—nature will diminish the birds until they balance with the cover and food. But for right now, you have quite a number of pheasants crammed into small patches of cover with bad weather coming on.

In such situations, a small party of visiting hunters can do well. Two or three men and a dog or two have an advantage they didn't have earlier in the year. First, the birds are not always eager to leave cover where they've established residence, because they seem to know that there are no other good spots around. Secondly, such cover patch is easier to spot because there is just so little of it compared to the way things were before wind, snow, and ice conspired to flatten things. Lastly, it's fairly easy to get permission to hunt because the landowner normally has his crops in and you aren't going to hurt anything tromping around.

The bad part about late hunting is that you could get yourself into a blizzard that shuts everything down and ruins your trip. Or the temperatures could plummet and make it just too miserable to hunt. Again—tradeoffs.

Let me tell you something about prairie blizzards. If you live in the East, you may think you're familiar with bad weather. I've lived in Iowa and have hunted all of the major states in that part of the country in weather that's horrible. I hunted once in Iowa when the chill factor was 50 below zero and the safety on my double froze up. So I'm telling

A morning's bag laid out after an English-style driven-bird shoot in
Denmark. Today Americans are found in nearly every party open to such
shoots on a pay basis. Before signing on, though, make sure you know
the costs to the penny *and* how many birds are to be "presented over the
guns." (Bryan Bilinski photo)

you this: if you haven't spent time on the plains when an
Alberta clipper is frolicking through, you have no idea of the
fury and life-threatening force these gales carry. I mean,
you can be a 21-year-old all-state football player and hate
tobacco and Scotch whiskey, and one of these storms will
kill you deader than a smelt. They're nothing to fool with.

Costwise, the out-of-stater has to factor in licenses and
stamps, food, lodging, and gas. Then, depending upon how
long he stays and how well he likes to eat and sleep, the
cost can run anywhere from a couple hundred dollars to
nearly a thousand. If you divide cost by the number of birds
you can legally shoot, a bird gets expensive—and even more
so when you figure it on the number of pheasants you *do*
shoot. But it's an experience. Besides, if we counted too
closely, nobody would hunt anything.

Here's a listing of general regulations and where to write for info in the four plains states, as of the 1985 season. Things change, though, so this is only advisory.

SOUTH DAKOTA

Game, Fish, & Parks

Sigurd Anderson Bldg.
Pierre, SD 47501-3185

Season: October 19–December 8 (with some exceptions)

Shooting Hours: Noon to sunset through October, 10 a.m. to sunset for remainder of season

Bag Limits: 3 a day, 15 in possession

Licenses/stamps: $57 (nonresident)

IOWA

Department of Natural Resources

Wallace State Office Bldg.
Des Moines, IA 50319

Season: November 2–January 5

Shooting Hours: 8 a.m.–4:40 p.m.

Bag Limits: 3 a day, 9 in possession

Licenses/stamps: $50.50

NEBRASKA

Game & Parks Commission

P.O. Box 30370
Lincoln, NE 68503

Season: November 2–January 15

Shooting Hours: one-half hour before sunrise to sunset until January 1. After that, shooting ends at 4 p.m.

Bag Limits: 3 a day, 9 in possession

Licenses/stamps:$47.50

KANSAS

Fish & Game Commission

Box 54A, RR2
Pratt, KS 67124

Season: November 9–January 31

Shooting Hours: one-half hour before sunrise to sunset

Bag Limits: 4 a day, 16 in possession

Licenses/stamps: $50.50

As you can see, unless you plan to eat or give away some of your birds, some states, specifically Iowa and Nebraska, lend themselves to shorter trips than others. If you get your limit each day for three days, you'll have your possession limit and will have to leave, stop hunting, or start eating. In South Dakota and Kansas, you have the chance for a longer hunt without worrying about having too many birds in possession.

Since most out-of-staters choose to bring home all of their birds, three-day hunts in Iowa or Nebraska make more sense than extended stays. Remember, though, that when you clean birds for the trip home, they must retain something that identifies them as rooster pheasants—a head or a leg with the spur intact is usually suggested.

VI
MISCELLANY

If any of us were good at arithmetic and could figure out what gamebirds cost per pound, we probably wouldn't hunt. At least, we wouldn't hunt pheasants.

PLANTED BIRDS

In some states in the East, planted birds are about the only pheasants that hunters get a chance at. Going by various names, this put-and-take hunting has proven itself in most places to be a waste of time and money, both of which might better be put into acquiring habitat to ensure long-term, natural propagation.

In Michigan I've hunted put-and-take pheasants a couple of times. About the only draw it had for me was that it opened earlier than the regular pheasant season. Evidently, I wasn't the only one so enticed, because every morning, alongside the roads bordering the state land where the birds had been released, the orange hats looked like Christmas lights on the Public Works building.

At promptly 8 a.m. the army would assault the fields, taking both the hens (legal) and the cocks that had been released. Normally, these birds were right in or near the ditches that followed the road, and they were easy pickin's. Within an hour, the birds had been cleaned out and the hunters were gone.

I saw a lot of illegalities—the chief offense being that the leg tags provided with the special put-and-take license were not always applied to the downed birds, or were applied with a feather between the sticky parts so the tag could later be removed in the comfort of the shooter's home for reuse later. A cute trick, but stupid and unsportsmanlike.

I also saw parties of hunters following other folks' dogs, birds shot on the ground, people sprinkled with shot, and generally the same type of atmosphere you associate with following the hatchery truck on the opening day of trout season—everybody wanted his share. In fact, there was more talk of when the "drop" (release) was made than of wind conditions, guns, loads, or chokes. The whole thing seemed a lot like salmon snagging, so when the put-and-take program started to die in Michigan, I didn't go to the funeral. It gave a lot of folks a lot of fun, I suppose, but it cost a lot of money, the rearing of a pheasant costing the state a lot more than it does private industry.

There is no way that programs such as this should ever be confused with an orderly, well-run, sporting shooting preserve.

PRESERVES

H. G. Wells was right, and he didn't even know it. There *is* a time machine. It's called by a variety of names, but "shooting preserve" will do. I go to one on occasion because I like what I can do there with my imagination.

If your hunting days are all too short, the seasons skimpy, and your dog's days afield too precious and few, the shooting preserve gives you a chance to get in some hunts when the normal "wild" seasons are closed—for a fee, of course.

When I use a preserve, I like to do a lot of pretending. The one near my home looks for all the world like the rolling hills of Iowa, and the pheasants and quail are lively and wild. I can work a dog or a boy or test out the fit of a new gunstock without the sense of urgency that comes with wild hunting where one chance might be all you get in a day.

And if an out-of-state hunting trip is out of the question, a fellow can get quality hunting close to home with no more cash outlay than he would if he traveled toward yon horizon.

I like the mean days of March for a preserve hunt. The weather is starting to moderate a bit, but it stills looks, feels, and, with a little pretending, *becomes* November. Cover is down, so the birds are in the brush, which adds to the difficulty of shooting, making things more realistic. My dogs like the preserve. The fat they picked up over the winter makes their tongues loll after a while, which you'd think would teach them a lesson, but it doesn't.

My son Chris shot his first birds on a shooting preserve, and I expect his kid brother Jake will do the same once his time arrives. I have the feeling that the last ones I'll ever shoot will be on such a place, I hope sometime in the next century, after I'm forced to forego those steep, wild hillsides in the back-of-beyond.

Preserves take you back to when farming was sloppy, fencerows were wide, and cropfields were dirty with weeds. Many of us remember such places and times early in our shooting careers, when the opening day of pheasant season approached the proportions of a national holiday and relatives we hadn't seen in a year showed up for the big drives.

The days of March make hunters long for November, and at a shooting preserve, you can do something about it. On an early-spring day, two gunners get ready for the bird their low-tailed Irish setter is pointing. (MI DNR photo)

Today, only at a preserve can you find the intimate sur-
roundings and the company restricted to what you want it
to be, and memories can wander back to the old days.
Shooting preserves don't detract from our normal hunting;
they add to it, giving it almost a historic dimension.

As far as the pheasant shooter goes, there isn't much
that is given away in terms of sport on a well-run preserve. I
may be getting older, but it seems to me that the birds I
hunt on preserves are as wild as the birds I hunted as a kid.
It seems strange, but when a fellow goes out of state to hunt
pheasants, he wants large numbers and tame birds—birds
that will stay put, cooperate with his dog, and offer him fair
chances. Yet when that same man goes to a preserve, he
often is critical of birds that are too domesticated, too "easy."

But on the preserves I've used, the ringnecks are very
wild—somtimes too wild. True, there are operations where
the manager will take the bird from the pen, wring its neck,
and hand it to you if that's what you want. But the guys
who run almost all the successful places are outdoorsmen
themselves—hunters and dog men—and unsporting conditions fly in the face of their personal ethics.

Speaking of dogs, preserves often will board your dog,
maybe even work him for you, and they probably will have a
selection of dogs that you can hunt with if your own is on
the mend or you're temporarily dogless.

The main criticism of preserves is the fact that you
have to pay for the birds, and, unlike England or Europe,
this goes against the grain of our Yankee pride. Well, do you
pay now? Let's take a look.

If you travel from an eastern state to, say, Iowa to hunt
pheasants, what will you have to shell out? At 1986 prices,
here goes:

Nonresident license and habitat stamp: $50.50
Food: $20 a day per man (if you eat cheap)
Lodging: $15 a day per man if you share a room
Gas: at least $50 if you share with another (a variable
here).

A well-run preserve will have dogs available for members and guests, with several breeds represented. For a hunter with little time for dog training—or room to keep a dog—this is an important feature.

Let's say that you stay three days and shoot your legally allowable nine birds, all you can bring back. The total tab—and this is a bare-bones cost excluding visits to the pub that the Storm and Strife doesn't know about—is $205.50.

Divide that by your nine birds, and you can see that each bird is going to cost you just a tad shy of $23—and that's if you take the limit.

There are constants that you'll pay either out of state or on a preserve: costs of guns, shells, clothing, and so forth. At this rate, a $15 pheasant taken on a preserve is actually a good deal.

Now, the best part is that you can take that same $205.50, spend it at a preserve, and end up stretching your trip over a few weeks by going a day at a time. Whenever I go hunting out of state, and I do so about five times a year, the third day out is a killer. The dog is tired, I'm tired, the anticipation is gone, the adrenaline is used up, and I basically loaf for a day in the middle. Once the well-known Second Wind comes along, I'm ready for the last couple of days of a five-day trip. Now, really, that middle day is wasted. As we get up in years/pounds/arthritis, we have to count on a rest day. Hunting should be fun—don't kill yourself.

A preserve pheasant, properly reared with a minimum of human contact and conditioned in flight pens, quickly reverts to the wild and becomes a challenging adversary. The grounds are usually groomed especialy for these birds, with an eye toward over-wintering cover.

I like to take my dog and walk the preserve grounds, hunting birds that have escaped other hunters. You can usually negotiate with the manager on the price of these birds—you both know they have been paid for already by the guy who had them released originally. Maybe you can hunt on a no birds, no pay arrangement, although the proprietor may want you to come across with a small fee because you're underfoot.

Some preserves are open to the public, while others have a private membership, with dues and maybe an initiation fee. The latter are probably the higher-quality places because often the members are better heeled and more discerning, not that the two always go together. The poshest preserves are those owned by a corporation and operated as an executive retreat/meeting center/entertainment spa. There, breaking even is not important, because the whole thing's a tax dodge in the first place.

The club I belong to has the following arrangements, but I had to look long and hard to find such an operation:

- Pheasants are released on a custom basis, with a set charge per bird released. The club owners have no way of knowing how good a shot you are, so paying only for birds you shoot is usually out of the question.

• Birds that have escaped—and there are always some around—can be hunted. No fee is charged for the hunting, and the fee for birds taken this way is lower than for birds custom-released;

• Other species are available—quail and chukars. The chukars, not native to my state, can be hunted all year on a licensed preserve.

• Birds are reared on the premises, and they get a few weeks in the flight pens before their scheduled release.

• The grounds offer excellent ruffed grouse and woodcock shooting. There is no charge for hunting or shooting these species, but the state-set seasons must be observed, not the longer shooting-preserve season.

• The club will bill you for your birds if you wish (a good deal if your wife doesn't open your mail).

• Facilities include 600 acres of land—parties are limited in each area, so the feeling of being alone is there.

• Buildings include a small sport shop, dining room, and lounge.

All in all, a shooting club, with pheasants the main lure, makes sense in the fast-track '80s.

GEAR

A number of items can make pheasant hunting a much more enjoyable sport. I'm not going to try to dictate what you should wear or carry with you, but merely make some suggestions.

Besides your gun or guns, your next most important piece of equipment is a pair of solid boots. I like leather most of the time because I've got crummy ankles, but the Bean type, with leather top and rubber-bottom also serves

Author with a pair of roosters taken from a stand of pines where they had sought cover. Most pheasant hunters believe in going light, even in wintry conditions. Because of the strenuous exercise, only a light vest and light brush pants are required. Gun is a light 12 bore of game-gun design with a very straight stock, which not only throws the pattern high to compensate for rising roosters, but also throws the recoil straight back rather than *up* and back, making it a comfortable gun to shoot—even with maximum-load shells—despite its six-pound weight.

well. Make sure the sole won't slip, and try to keep the boots as waterproof as possible, because some of the places the birds frequent, especially late in the season, are damned wet. When it's *real* wet, I wear knee-high rubber boots.

A pair of brush pants with nylon facing help you slip through the blackberry canes with a minimum of blood loss. If you're hunting right, you'll wear a pair out in a year, maybe sooner, regardless of what the makers tell you.

British oiled-cotton, "thornproof" clothing like this jacket from Barbour is about the best protection there is for *all* wet weather during the season. Light and "breathable," it's almost indestructible. (Bryan Bilinski photo)

A good hat is a must. It keeps the hair/wind/dust/sweat out of your eyes, and it keeps your head dry. Most folks like the ball cap style, but I like the tweed models with a two-inch brim snapped down all around. If the bill of a ball cap is too long, you have to pick your head up to see the mark over a gun barrel. You do it without thinking, shoot high, and wonder why.

In many places, blaze orange is the law of the land, and where it isn't, it's a good idea anyway. I usually stitch on a strip of this material as an extra-wide hatband, and it shows up well, especially in low-light conditions.

A shooting vest carries all you'll need for a day in the fields. In mine, I have shells, doggie treats, Smitty treats (for me, that is), a first-aid kit for the dog, and a pocket knife. But vests aren't all that great when the winds of November start howling, so I switch to one of the British thornproof coats. I have two that I especially like. One is called the Beaufort, made by Barbour, and it has a full game bag. The other is a longer one made by Hogg's of Fife that I use when it's raining because it keeps my legs dry.

Oiled cotton clothing such as this is the standard in the British Isles, where lousy weather is a fact of shooting life. These items shed water and wear better than any synthetic product I'm familiar with, and given a fresh coating of the wax material every couple of years, they'll be useful a lot longer than *you* will be. They cut the wind and turn the water, and yet are light, and they're designed for shotgunners—beat that.

I carry my shells, a lunch, and some odds and ends in a leather-and-canvas shooting bag with a shoulder strap, and on the bag I have clamped a bird strap, one of these leather arrangements that you loop around the head of a bird. The strap and birds can be hung up so the birds cool naturally in the wind. The bag stays in the car, of course, until needed.

The pheasant hunter should borrow from his grouse-hunting brothers—or his own grouse-hunting gear—and get a good pair of shooting glasses. In yellow, they heighten contrast and brighten things on dreary days, and in the brush they can save your baby blues from a bad twigging. Once you scratch a cornea, you'll wish you'd had the glasses, but by then it's a little late.

And try a good pair of leather or cloth shooting gloves. Get the kind that will give your wrists some protection from clutching briars. You'll be more comfortable and you'll shoot better.

Many shooters like to draw their birds immediately after dropping them. I don't, because normally it's cool enough so that spoilage isn't a problem. Besides, a bird with an empty body cavity stuck into a grimy game bag can probably pick

Bird straps such as this one hold rooster pheasants by the head, allowing natural cooling of the body. Although many shooters like to draw their birds in the field, care must be taken to make sure that the body cavity is then kept clean—a tricky task under hunting conditions. Birds can be hung for a day from the strap in a cool place, thus tenderizing them for the table.

up more germs than a batch of conventioneers in Atlantic City.

Instead, I hang the birds from the strap outside where they can cool. Birds hung for a day or two taste better to me, the hanging causing meat fibers to age and break down. Also, you'll be surprised at how much easier it is to face the cleaning chores the next day, after you've had a chance to rest your bones a bit.

There's some misconception about hanging game in

this country, so I'll tell you the way I do it: don't touch the body cavity until you're ready to clean the bird—unless the bird is badly shot up. In England and Europe, some folks hang a bird until it decays to the point that the head and neck separate—it's time to clean 'em when you find 'em on the floor. Not me.

MAPS

Using maps is a fine way of locating potential hunting grounds, especially in strange areas. I like the U.S. Geological Survey's 7½-minute quadrangle maps. I laminate them with plastic and then write on them with grease pencils. The maps are available for a few dollars each from the U.S. Geological Survey. If you want maps for areas east of the Mississippi, write:

Eastern Distribution Branch

U.S. Geological Survey

1200 South Eads St.

Arlington, VA 22202

For areas west of the Mississippi, write:

Western Distribution Branch

U.S. Geological Survey

Building 41, Federal Center

P.O. Box 25286

Denver, CO 80225

These maps show elevations, land formations, swamps, rivers, lakes, intermittent waterways (streams that run, say, only in the spring), and man-made structures such as dams and buildings—at least those existing when the aerial surveys were made. By using these maps, you can find pockets of cover or potential cover that may not be visible from roads—next best thing to an aerial photo.

Today's pheasant hunter should spend a lot of time poring over maps, looking for likely pockets of cover that can hold birds on land accessible to him. Plat maps, state game department maps, topographic maps, and a record of his past years' successes and failures are all important in making the most of a man's limited amount of time afield. (Photo by Tom Carney)

Plat maps are useful as well. These are put out by counties in many states and show parcels of land and—more importantly—who owns them. Sometimes a plat map, especially in the East, will tell you that a juicy-looking piece of acreage is public property. Such pockets of municipally owned land are more common than people think.

I like looking for the intermittent streams symbol on topo maps because I've had good luck finding cover that way. The symbol, usually a broken line, almost always follows an area of low elevation such as a gulley, and the likelihood of standing water may well mean that the farmer has pretty much left it alone—it's too steep and wet to farm, especially in the spring.

You'll have to get out of the car to check such areas out, but if you spot a tree line near the intermittent (sometimes called "vernal," for springtime) stream, you may be in business because the trees indicate that everybody has left the place alone for a long time. When I was in college, an instructor who was a rabid pheasant man taught me this little trick with topos. He'd say: "Show me standing water in the spring, and I'll show you pheasants in the fall." I always remembered that, though I've forgotten much of what he tried to teach me in class.

SOME OPINIONS

Because I trust the judgment of some folks, and also because you spent good money for this book (or hooked it from somebody who did), I thought you'd like to receive the benefit of the knowledge of recognized experts in the field. So I asked some experts who are also friends to give you their thoughts about techniques, dogs, and guns. Here goes:

JIM WOOLEY ON TACTICS:—Jim Wooley is a resident of Iowa and a Field Representative with Pheasants Forever. I mention Jim elsewhere in this book, but I should also tell you that prior to joining PF, he was part of the pheasant-management team for the Iowa Conservation Commission. He knows pheasants as few others do.

Jim is a strong advocate of hunting according to conditions, especially wind conditions, feeling that a hunter's ability to use wind wisely can cut down a lot on the propensity pheasants have toward running.

"If you are moving against the wind," he says, "you are far more likely to get up on a bird and have him hold than if you're coming *with* the wind. With the wind, he can hear you coming a half mile away, and he's going to get up and go. Pheasants and quail and partridge and turkeys are all light-breasted birds; they're not particularly inclined to fly if they don't have to. [Ducks and other strong-flying birds have darker meat because their breasts carry a greater blood supply.] The walking and running trait is there in the bird already, and I don't think hunting pressure has caused a greater number of runners than we would normally have anyway.

"Right now, as I write this, we've got a good example of this here in Iowa. It's early December, and there's crusty snow. It's just impossible to get up on a bird unless you've got a windy day and you're going against the wind, working into cover that's fairly heavy so that the birds hold.

"I have a Labrador retriever—a flushing dog, a close worker—and generally I just search for good-looking cover and try to work with the conditions. I try to move into the wind, giving my dog a chance to work so that the birds aren't running clear out the end of the cover.

"More often than not, I like to work idle, permanent cover, like wide waterways and ditches, that is near cropland. I'm not an aficionado of standing corn. First, you can't get close to a bird in that stuff. Second, my dog doesn't work well for me in standing corn, and third, if you're hunting with a party, it can be a dangerous situation."

Wooley is very hopeful that the Farm Bill will do a lot for pheasants by providing the habitat they need. His organization is certainly going to grow as vegetation plantings are done under the Conservation Reserve provisions of the bill, starting with what could be several millions of acres of prospective nesting cover. Wooley notes that it will be several years before the set-aside acreage matures enough to provide winter cover, but given the Farm Bill's long life, that shouldn't be a problem after a couple of years.

GENE HILL ON GUNS:—Gene Hill is a friend of mine of many years. He is known throughout the sporting world for his writings in *Field & Stream* and *Gun Dog* magazines, and for his many books. A thoughtful, reflective man,

Hilly is also a world-class shotgunner, his claims to the contrary notwithstanding. He's also an experienced pheasant shooter with definite views on what constitutes good guns and loads for pheasants.

"The perfect pheasant gun depends on some things. For example, when I was training dogs, I shot a full/full 12 gauge double. It worked fine—I could control the dog and still kill the birds because I had a lot of time before the birds were out of range.

"So if your dogs are a little wild and you're in big country, I would use a lot of choke and big shot, like 4s and 5s. Normally, I'd say modified and full in a double, modified—and a tight modified—in a pump or autoloader, shot no smaller than 6s, and 12 gauge, 3¼-dram, 1¼-ounce loads. Anything bigger or hotter, and you'll lose your pattern.

"I'd have the gun stocked pretty straight. A pheasant is a rising bird, and the tendency is to shoot under unless you've got a gun that will shoot a little high."

I asked Hilly what differences he notes when shooting pheasants as compared with quail and grouse, and he told me, "Pheasants are larger, Smith." Then, seriously, he added: "It doesn't make any difference if you body-shoot a quail, grouse, or dove; but if you body-shoot a pheasant, you may lose it. So you want to be as "head conscious' with pheasants as you'd be with waterfowl."

DAVE DUFFEY ON DOGS:—Dave is a dog writer and dog trainer, and has hunted pheasants in virtually every state in which they live. He is known through his books and through his various training columns, which appear in several outdoor publications, notably the Sportsman Group magazines and *Gun Dog*.

"What am I looking for in a pheasant dog?" he says. "A dog that'll find pheasants!" (Another wise guy!)

"No, let's see—it has to be a particularly aggressive dog. That's the most important thing. Unless the dog is aggressive, he isn't going to pin his birds. You'll get a creepy, crawly, eternally relocating sort of performance from a non-aggressive member of a pointing breed; if it's a flushing dog, it won't move fast enough to get the birds up. Very often, wild flushes will occur with such dogs, rather than in front of the dog that really dashes in and flushes them quickly.

"With a pointing dog, if he's real bold and aggressive, sometimes he seems to mesmerize the bird. Pheasants are a tough bird for a pointing dog to handle, but the way he's got to handle them is slam-bang and pin 'em, and that's it. If he walks or creeps in, the bird keeps moving and the dog keeps relocating, pointing, relocating, pointing, and the first thing you know, you've walked across an 80-acre field and haven't seen a bird."

What are his favorite breeds—one, two, three—for pheasants? "Springer spaniel first, Labrador retriever second, and if I wanted one of the pointing breeds, chances are most people would be most satisfied with one of the short-tailed dogs—one of the German, Continental breeds (German shorthair, wirehair, etc.). I actually think, though, that an English pointer or English setter—a good one, mind you—will do better on pheasants if he's broke to them.

DAVE MEISNER ON COVER:—Dave, another friend of many years, and I usually manage to hunt together for a few days each season in Iowa. Dave founded *Gun Dog* Magazine in the early 1980s and after he sold it, he took up a life largely centering on hunting, especially pheasants.

"When it comes to cover, I look for the thickest I can find, especially stuff like multiflora rose that borders cropfields—particularly grain. But the crop has to be down, especially if its corn, because otherwise you'll be wasting your time—the birds will just slip out into the standing corn ahead of you, and you'll never get a chance at them.

"I like hunting in rainy weather. Good dog work is important to me, and in damp, misty weather my dogs (a French Brittany and a German wirehair) give me really super points. The birds hold tighter, and I'm sure scenting is better, too. Speaking of dog work, retrieving is what makes a finished dog, and it's what makes a real *pheasant* dog.

Without that ability, you'll lose birds—and don't kid yourself that you won't.

"Late in the season, I look for the same type of cover—really thick stuff. Actually, it has to be even thicker than earlier in the year to withstand what the weather has done to it up until then. If you take a look at a brushy November ditchbank and then look at it again in December, it'll be entirely different. Even with no hunters, birds are going to be spooky simply because there are few places to hide."

Dave, who knows a lot about dogs, says that there are few "purists" among pheasant dog men because pheasant hunters shoot any roosters their dogs put up, even birds flushed accidentally or after a busted point. Unlike quail hunters, we just don't have enough birds to shoot only those our dogs handle well.

MISTAKES

In any hunting situation, the hunter can make many mistakes, the hunted only one. Well, pheasant hunters make their share of mistakes, and the birds make few—one good reason that more birds are not brought to hand.

I've listed some of the common ones, those that seem to me to be the miscues made most often by the rank and file—me included.

TALKING—The sound of the human voice is death to good hunting. The typical pheasant is hatched, lives, dodges predators, feeds, suffers through winter storms, and finally dies right in the heart of civilization. A bird of farm country, he hears tractors, combines, cars and trucks out on the four-lane, the noon whistle from the fire station, and even gunshots during the season. What he almost never hears is the sound of a human voice. Few voices carry far enough to reach him, unless that voice comes from somebody tromping through his habitat—a hunter.

Bird hunters talk, even if they try not to. Pheasant

hunters seem to talk more than any other bird seekers, normally because three or four people hunt together; the average pheasant-hunting party is bigger than, say, the average batch of grouse or quail hunters. So the chances of talking are greater. We gab about the football game, the weather, how to hunt this or that piece of cover; we holler at the dog, whoop it up when we nail a bird, say hiya to the local farmer. And all of these things have a detrimental effect on our ability to get close to birds.

First, you should have a set of hand signals that all members of your party understand. A low whistle gets the attention of the other members, and then the hand signals take over: "Swing around," "Come straight through," "The dog's on point/making game," "Circle ahead, a bird's running"—all of these can be translated into hand signals so that you don't alert birds.

Similarly, your dog should understand some basic hand signals for quartering, checking in, scouting out pieces of cover that you can see but he can't, and so forth.

Be sure to minimize the talking—it lets the birds know exactly where you are—exactly what you *don't* want.

WORKING TRANSIENT COVER—I'm referring here to the type of cover that is seasonal—present in the summer and fall, but absent in the spring and winter, when pheasants need nesting cover and protective cover, respectively.

I don't know how many times I've seen parties of shooters tromping across a picked cornfield, their guns held expectantly at port-arms, awaiting a flush that will never come because the nearest good—permanent—cover is a half mile away.

If you have the time, the best season to scout pheasant cover is the winter, when you can get a good idea of what's standing and what's not. Look for brushy woodlots, railroad grades, field terraces, ditch banks, creekbeds, and so on— the all-year cover.

OUT-OF-CONTROL DOGS—An ill-mannered dog may be worse than none. A pheasant dog should be trained to stay in control; if he won't, he'll never make it. A pro trainer can get your dog tuned up if needed, and I elaborate a bit on this point in the chapter on dogs. But the truth is, most pheasant dogs work too big—too far out—for their skills at holding point or rousting a bird into the air. A dog that can hold a bird is a delight; one that wild-flushes birds should be left at home.

NOT HUNTING ACCORDING TO CONDITIONS— Weather, the condition of the cover, the wind—all these have an impact on how cover should be worked, or what cover should be worked.

On rainy days the birds are almost certain to be in thick stuff, not in high, open grassland. All cover should be worked into the wind, to give you and your dog the advantage. Cover that has been flattened by weather and thus offers less bird-holding potential has to be crossed off and new cover located. These are just some examples of hunting *with*, not against, the existing conditions.

NOT BLOCKING—All cover, every time, everywhere, should be blocked if you have the manpower. The greatest reason birds escape unscathed is that they head out ahead of hunters—out of gun range—and take a path of flight where no other hunters are located. Your object is to subliminally "herd" any birds present toward an area where they 1) must fly because they've run out of cover, and 2) will flush over one of your party positioned for a shot. Yet time after time we hunt fields without giving a thought to where any out-of-range flushers will head. Block, block, block.

To show some of these common mistakes, and also to take a look at some of the things we can do right, let's follow some hypothetical hunters into the field for a pheasant hunt. It's the second weekend of the season. The weather has been dry, the autumn rains being late this year. Our cast of characters assembles at the coffee shop in a Midwest town, a farming community set among the hills and fields of Iowa—but it could be anywhere.

Jerry, Bryan, and Tom are swilling coffee and boasting about their respective dogs. Jerry and Tom have pointing dogs—shorthairs—and Bryan owns and uses Labs. Like all pheasant hunters who are dog men, they spend a lot of time bragging about their animals, both the breed and their own individuals.

Finally, after an hour of banter and fun, Jerry glances at his watch and announces that the birds should be up and about, and the gang should do the same, so the hunters stroll to the car and head for the first field.

It is about 9:30 when the hunters arrive at a farm where Jerry has permission to hunt. They park their car on a lane, load the guns, pocket the keys, and head into a field of foxtail grass, ideal roosting cover for pheasants. Jerry had good luck there hunting by himself last week, hitting the field first thing in the morning.

Found any mistakes yet? Well, let's look. First, the guys spent far too much time drinking coffee and talking. If their first hunt of the day was intended to be in roosting cover, they should have been in the field at legal shooting time, which was 8 a.m., not 9:30. The birds are up and have headed for feed, so the first swing through the field is bound to be unproductive. Last week Jerry, hunting alone, got good shooting because he got up early and went hunting; he didn't spend the productive early-morning hours in the diner.

Second mistake: even though Jerry had permission, he should have introduced his friends to the farmer, and he shouldn't have parked the car on a farm lane, a lane the autumn-busy farmer is bound to use sometime during the day. If he had to park there, he should have left the keys in the car for the farmer. The chances are good that they will be called back to move the car, or an angry farmer caught in a farm-machinery gridlock will be waiting by their car when they come back.

Mistake No. 3: in dry conditions, dogs do their best work in the morning, when dew and residual moisture from the night before carry bird scent better. Now the dogs are fighting a dry wind—because the wind always blows in Iowa after the sun's been up for a while.

As they hunt across the field, which follows the slope of a hill toward a creek gulley, the boys watch their dogs working, Jerry and Tom bragging about their animals' ground coverage, Bryan calling attention to how his busy Lab checks out each piece of potential cover. A pastoral scene, repeated hundreds of times this day across pheasant range.

But a mistake nonetheless. The talking is alerting any birds still in the foxtail or nearby that the hunt is on and exactly where the men are heading. And the hunters are working toward the creek gulley, thereby pushing birds right toward where they want to go anyway. Birds must be pushed to where they don't *want to be.*

The hunters arrive at the creekbank. On one side, a cornfield is still standing; on the other is a picked field. The men fan out three abreast and work the creek bed toward the east.

Spot some more errors? Sure. The unpicked field is a natural escape route for the birds. Better if the hunters worked half the gulley, the part along the picked field, placing one of the guys (probably Bryan and his Lab) at the end as a blocker. But which end? They should be working the gulley from the east toward the west, not the other way around—for two reasons. First, heading east puts the prevailing wind at their and their dogs' backs, and in the pheasants' faces, giving the birds the hearing advantage, and with the racket the hunters are making, that's enough to tip off the township. Second, heading east puts the sun in their faces, making identification of a cock pheasant difficult and the shooting even more so.

A few straggling birds in the creek gulley, however, do hold for the boys. One bird goes up in front of Bryan's dog, and he misses, his 12 gauge pump coming into play a little too slowly. By the time the others can react, the bird is gone, not out of range but out of sight in the thick cover. Other birds flush wild ahead.

Bryan's full-choked pump, being a bit heavy, ill-balanced, and overchoked, is out of sync for the cover being worked. Bryan, with a Lab, should be using a gun with more open choke and better balanced for fast handling in thick cover, the places pheasants live these days. The shot was a quick one in thick cover, and Bryan's gun, which is dandy for open fields, was just wrong for the conditions; Bryan tried a pitch-and-run with a three-wood. No wonder he missed. The commotion pushed birds into the air that were running ahead because they knew the boys were there. The shooting just made 'em move a little faster.

The hunters decide they should send a blocker ahead to guard the spot where the creek gulley crosses the road, a place where birds, pinched between the road and the hunters, should jump into the air. Tom goes ahead, walking the border where the picked cornfield meets the creek gulley. He stands and waits, signalling with his hat that he's ready. Jerry and Bryan move through, but no birds jump as they push the last bits of cover and meet up with Tom.

Good plan, but poorly carried out. Tom should have been sent to the end before the drive of the creek bed even began (realizing that they were working the creek in the wrong direction in the first place). Instead, they waited until less than 100 yards separated the "pinch point" from the drivers. Then Tom walked far too close to the creek bed and on the picked-cornfield side, thus alerting birds to his presence and pushing them up into the standing corn on the other side of the gulley. It would have been far better if Tom had been sent in a wide circle to the end, or even if he had tromped carefully through the unpicked corn to get into position. That way, his movement may have pushed some escaping birds back into the creek gulley and wouldn't have alerted those already there.

At the end of the creek-bed push, the boys stop to talk things over and decide that the birds have probably already moved out of roosting cover into the feeding areas, and are back in the thick cover.

Aha! Now they're starting to think. It's close to 11 a.m., and the birds probably are *in the thick stuff.*

Jerry suggests a woodlot on the other side of the picked field, so they set off.

A long walk across ground that's not productive— right, guys? Given some better planning, they wouldn't have had to make that fruitless forced march.

Arriving at the edge of the woodlot, Bryan takes charge, asking Jerry what's on the other side. Jerry tells him that the other side, the west side of the woodlot, has a brushy edge that abuts a plowed field. Bryan starts to think and— correctly—deduces that any birds in the woods will be pushed west, into the wind and thus to the dogs' advantage, and will hold in the brush rather than fly across or run across the barren field.

The hunters enter the woods, which opens up like a park, with very little ground cover. Jerry, Tom, and their shorthairs quickly cover the open ground. Bryan, meandering behind his fastidious little Lab, lags behind. Suddenly he is startled by gunfire from Jerry and Tom's direction. They are shooting at rooster pheasants, but the birds have flushed far ahead of them, and they had little chance. Bryan slowly strolls to the edge of the field and watches as his Lab starts getting birdy. She pushes out first one hen, then another, and then, from almost under Bryan's feet, a fat rooster cackles his way into the air, rising straight up to cut back across the top of the woodlot rather than try to make his break across the open field. Bryan waits for the bird to top out, and drops him.

All right! The success resulted from Bryan's taking his time. The plan was right—the birds would have to move ahead of the hunters, and probably would hold in the brush on the west side of the woodlot. The men even worked the wind right.

But the two shorthairs, not being under control, raced across what they saw as unproductive, open woods and got into birds while their owners were still too far away. And Jerry and Tom compounded the error by racing ahead after their dogs. If they had walked slowly, the dogs, even though on the far edge of control, might have settled down and held their points. But with bird scent in their noses and their owners beating feet to catch up, the dogs felt pressured and rushed, and bumped their birds.

On the other hand, Bryan's Lab, working foot scent across the woodlot, had to take her time, and so the birds did not sense the danger until Bryan was within good range. The best move of all, of course, was the plan to push toward a place where the birds would not run and probably wouldn't fly until forced: the plowed field. Finally, Bryan, learning from his earlier miss in the thick creek bed, held his fire until the bird topped out and his pattern had a chance to open up.

The boys now have one bird in hand, and it's getting on toward noon. With no other cover available, they decide to recross the picked field, cross the creek, and work a section of the unpicked corn back to the car. This they do, and the dogs run in the field, pushing up a number of birds 100 yards out. Arriving back at the car, they get in it and head for the diner and lunch.

That final exercise was a waste of time and energy. The dogs ran about pointlessly in the corn, the noon sun and wind having eliminated any chance of good scenting. The hunters should have simply strolled back to the car to conserve energy. Now their dogs are tired, and so are they. You can't shoot birds if you're too tired to hunt.

Back at the diner, they make plans, something they should have done in the morning. Nobody's bragging about his dog now.

Tom knows a place to hunt, he says, so they haul a napkin out of the dispenser, and Tom sketches the layout: a gulley with no water, but it's too low to farm and thus has been left alone. This gulley runs east and west. The west end stops at a county road, the east end at a picked bean field. Bryan, the planner, takes over.

He says that he and Jerry will drop Tom off silently where the gulley crosses the county road. Tom is to walk down into the gulley far enough so that he is off the road right-of-way and can therefore legally hunt. Jerry and Bryan will then circle with the car back to where the bean field starts. They will work the edges of the field, where birds are likely to be feeding, and they will *slowly and silently* push those edges toward where they converge and blend into the gulley. Then they will work slowly and silently along the gulley toward Tom's position. By working in this way, Bryan deduces, they will push birds out of the feeding field into cover, and toward an obstruction—the road—where they will be more likely to fly.

Nice job! The boys looked at the layout on paper and took into consideration the following important factors, things they had overlooked that morning: the wind direction (they'll be working west, into the wind, and the sun shouldn't be a problem since it's still high in the sky), what the birds are likely to be doing (feeding), where (the bean field's edges), the need for stealth and silence (always), and the wisdom of placing a shooter where he will have a chance once the birds decide they must fly.

Back at the bean field, Bryan looks far ahead and sees Tom's orange hat. He's ready. Bryan signals across to Jerry, and the two men slowly work their edges toward where they funnel into the gulley. Bryan's Lab roots a rooster into the air out of some high grass at the field edge, and Bryan drops it. Jerry's shorthair has a runner nailed where the bird tried to cut north away from the field edge and ran out of cover. Jerry grasses the bird at close range.

Now they are in the gulley. The dogs at first have their heads in the air, testing the breeze. Bryan's Lab drops her head down to the ground and her tail is waving—birds running ahead. Bryan ducks out to the gulley edge and shows Tom their position. When the hunters get 30 yards apart, birds, pinched between them, come into the air. Tom shoots the first bird, misses another, reloads, pulls off an illegal hen, and drops his second rooster. Jerry shoots one that comes out low and crossing, and Bryan follows his dog, which is chasing a runner that tried to cut between the drivers when the shooting started. The bird panics, though, and Bryan collects his limit.

Fine job. The men shot six roosters on that drive after bagging only one in the morning because they stopped, sat down, and talked things over. But the trick was to analyze the cover, the conditions, and the birds. They did and scored. Let's hope they learned something!

PHEASANT HUNTING COMPETITIONS

Pheasants seem to lend themselves to competition. In many of the important springer spaniel trials, pheasants are used rather than pigeons, the better to test the breed of dog on the species of bird he was born to seek.

In some of the "shooting trials" for hunters and their dogs, such as those put on by the National Shoot To Retrieve Association, pheasants are used, but normally less-expensive quail are the target. These trials require the dog to find, point, and retrieve a bird; the handler/owner has to shoot the bird.

At last report, semi-annual pheasant-hunting championships are held in Goose Lake, Iowa—one in the spring, one in the fall—that feature pheasants exclusively. This event is one of the type of competitions that are as follows:

Six birds are released into a field. Two men and a dog— the team—enter the field and in 30 minutes try to find and shoot as many of the birds as they can with the fewest shells. Each pheasant shot and recovered counts so many points, and each unused shell counts some more points.

Normally, I'm not a big fan of things like bass tournaments, betting $5 on who gets the next bird, and such. But these events are great sport because they are held in the off-season when you can't otherwise hunt, and the birds are pen-reared. Besides, many of the pheasants escape and populate the countryside.

And isn't that what we pheasant hunters really want?

APPENDIX: DIRECTORY OF PRESERVES

Here is a listing of hunting preserves, compiled by the North American Gamebird Association. I publish it here with the permission of NAGA. This list includes only those NAGA members that adhere to the following minimum standards as set forth by the Association:

1) The area should look like good hunting country, with a blend of natural and cultivated cover.

2) Pheasants, quail, and chukars should be full-plumaged, more than 16 weeks old, and the same color and conformation as birds in the wild.

3) Mallards should be similar in weight and plumage to free-ranging mallards and capable of strong flight between release sites and rest ponds.

4) Well-trained dogs should be available for guests and to reduce crippling losses of game.

If you'd like more information on NAGA and any of its books or magazines on gamebird propagation and development of improved, long-season hunting resorts, contact: Walter S. Walker, Secretary, NAGA, P.O. Box 2105, Cayce-West Columbia, SC 29171. The phone number is (803) 796-8163.

KEY TO THE DIRECTORY
P—Pheasants
Q—Quail
C—Chukar
T—Wild Turkey
M—Mallard
*—Open to the public
**—Membership only
***—Open to the public on both a day-shooting and a membership basis.
The months shown are each club's hunting seasons.

ALABAMA

Season: Pheasant—12 months
 Quail—October–March
License: In-state, $10
 Out-of-state, $15 and up

Elmore County
Wood's Gamebird Farm
Rt. 1, Box 181
Titus, AL 36080
(205) 567-7711
P,Q,T,* October–March

Talladega County
Selwood Farm & Hunting Preserve
Rt. 1, Box 230
Alpine, AL 35014
(205) 362-7595
Q,*** October 1–March 1

ARIZONA

Season: October 1–March 31.
License: No license required at commercial preserves.

Maricopa County
Salt Cedar Shooting Preserve
P.O. Box 1001
Buckeye, AZ 85326

(602) 386-2923
P,Q,C,Doves, Ducks*** October 1–March 31

ARKANSAS
Season: October 1–March 31
License: Special Preserve License $3/day; nonresident license $6

Conway County
Point Remove WMA
P.O. Box 133
Hattieville, AR 72063
(501) 354-0136
Q,P,T, Ducks, Doves*** October 1–March 31

Drew County
Arkansas Quail Farm & Hunting Resort
P.O. Box 301
Dermott, AR 71638
(501) 538-3196
P,Q,C,*** October 1–March 31

Nevada County
Nevada County Game Birds
Rt. 1, Box 171
Buckner, AR 71827
P,Q,C October 1–March 31
No license required

CALIFORNIA
Season: 114 days, varies by zone
License: In-state, $13.25/season
          Out-of-state, $6.25/day

Riverside County
Raahauge's Hunting Club
5800 Bluff St.
Norco, CA 91760
(714) 735-2361
P,D September 1–March 15

Tehama County
Red Bank Ale & Quail Game Bird Club
P.O. Box 627
Red Bluff, CA 96080
P,Q,* October 1–April 20

COLORADO

Season: All year
License: Out-of-state, $32.50

Elbert County
Jalmor Sportsmen's Club
Star Route Box 40
Ramah, CO 80832
(303) 541-2854
P,** All year

Larimer County
Rocky Ridge Sporting & Conservation Club
6221 N. City Rd. 15
Ft. Collins, CO 80524
(303) 482-8997
P,C,*** October 1–March 31

Western Wildlife Adventures
1322 Webster Ave.
Ft. Collins, CO 80524
(303) 221-3241
P,C,Q,*** All year

Weld County
Eagle's Nest Country
420 E. 58th Ave., Suite 155
Denver, CO 80216
(303) 295-1217
P,Q,C,Doves, Geese, Ducks** October 1–March 31

CONNECTICUT

Season: September 15–March 31
License: None required

Windham County
Markover Hunting Preserve
Cook Hill Rd.
Danielson, CT 06239
(203) 774-4116
P,C,* September 15–March 31

FLORIDA
Season: October 1–April 30
License: Nonresident license, $6

Holmes County
Thundering Wings Hunting Preserve
Rt. 2, Box 20C
Caryville, FL 32427
(904) 623-0725, 547-9520
Q,P,C,*** October 1–April 20

Thundering Wings Hunting Preserve
969 Lakeside Dr.
Milton, FL 32570
(904) 547-9520 & 623-0725
Q,P,C,*** October 1–April 20 (located in Bonifay)

GEORGIA
Season: October 1–March 31
License: Out-of-state, $10

Hancock County
Covey Rise Farm
Rt. 3
Mayfield, GA 31087
(404) 444-6739
P,Q,Doves,*** October 1–March 31

Harris County
Callaway Gardens Hunting Preserve
Hwy. 18 West
Pine Mountain, GA 31822
(404) 663-2281, ext. 129
Q,P,*** October 1–March 31

Miller County
Babcock Plantation & Quail Preserve
Michael R. Pullen
Rt. 2, Box 323
Babcock, GA 31737
(912) 758-5454
Q,Doves,Ducks,***

Mitchell County
Riverview Plantation
Rt. 2, Box 515
Camilla, GA 31730
(912) 294-4904
Q,*** October 1–March 31

Terrell & Calhoun County
Tallawahee Plantation
J.E. Bangs
Rt. 5, Box 204
Dawson, GA 31742
(912) 995-2265 or 995-4560
Q,*** October 1–March 31

HAWAII

Honolulu
Westbeach Game Preserve
P.O. Box 88537
Honolulu, HI 96815
(808) 395-4309
P,C,Q,T,*** All year

ILLINOIS
Season: September 1–April 15
License: Special nonresident, $5

Bureau County
Hickory Grove Hunting Club
Rt. 1
Wyanet, IL 61379

(815) 699-2603
P,Q,C,T,Ducks,** October 1–April 15
Grundy County
Senica Hunt Club
P.O. Box 306
Maywood, IL 60153
(362) 681-3999
Q,P,** September 1–April 15
Lee County
Briar Knoll Hunting Club
Rt. 1
Amboy, IL 61310
(815) 857-2320
P,Q,C,Ducks,*** September 1–April 15

Great Tey Chase
Rt. 1, Box 89
Rt. 26 & Union Rd.
Harmon, IL 61042
(312) 961-5510
P,Q,C,T,Deer,** September 1–April 15

McHenry County
Gypsy Glen Farms
30808 N. Darrell Rd.
McHenry, IL 60050
(815) 385-2144
P,Q,C,T,Doves,*** September 1–April 15

McCullom Lake Hunt Club
10603 Okeson Rd.
P.O. Box 303
Hebron, IL 60034
(815) 648-2775
P,Q,** September 1–April 15

Richmond Hunting Club
5016 Rt. 173
Richmond, IL 60071
(815) 678-3271
P,M,C,Q,T,*** September 1–April 15

Pike County
Hopewell Views Hunting Club
Rt. 2
Rockport, IL 62370
(217) 734-9234
P,Q,C,Doves,Deer,*** September 1–April 15

Washington County
Heggemeier Hunting Club
Rt. 2
Nashville, IL 62263
(618) 327-3709
Q,P,C,T,Wild Mallards*** September 1–April 15

INDIANA
Season: September 1–April 30
License: Special preserve, $6
         5-day regular nonresident, $10

LaPorte County
Seven Springs Club
0433 W. Rt. 20
LaPorte, IN 46350
(219) 326-8480
P,C,Geese,Doves,Wild Ducks** September 1–March 31

Owen County
Rolling Acres Hunt & Fish Clubs
R.R. 1, Box 5
Quincy, IN 47456
(317) 795-4444
P,Q,C,** September 1–April 30

So. Lake County
West Creek Resort
17207 State Line Rd.
Lowell, IN 46356
(219) 696-6752 or 696-6101
P,C,* September 1–April 30

IOWA

Season: September 1–March 31
License: Special nonresident, $5.25

Clinton County
Arrowhead Hunting & Conservation Club
Rt. 1, Box 28
Goose Lake, IA 52750
(319) 577-2267
P,C,Q,*** September 1–March 31

Jasper County
Oakview Hunting Club & Kennels
Rt. 2
Prairie City, IA 50228
(515) 994-2094
P,Q,C,M,*** September 1–March 31

KANSAS

Season: September 1–March 31
License: Special nonresident, $9.25

Elk County
Flint Oak Ranch
Rt. 1
Fall River, KS 67047
(316) 658-4401
P,Q,T,Doves,Ducks,** September 1–March 31

Ness County
McDonald Game Farm
107 S. Franklin
Ness City, KS 67560
(913) 798-2541
P,Q,* September 1–March 31

Ottawa County
Blue Line Club
Rt. 1, Box 139A
Solomon, KS 67480

(913) 488-3785
P,C,Q,* September 1–March 31

Wabaunsee County
Maike Hunting Club
R.R. 2, Box 152
Alma, KS 66401
(913) 765-3820
P,Q,C,T,*** September 1–March 31

Woodson County
Lone Pine Shooting Preserve
Rt. 1, Box 79
Toronto, KS 66777
(316) 637-2967
P,C,Q,* September 1–March 31

KENTUCKY
Season: September 1–May 15
License: Special nonresident, $7.50

Magaffin County
Hunters Paradise #2
Larry Allen
Harper, KY 41440
(606) 349-5977 or 743-1560
Q,C,P,*** September 1–May 15

Robertson County
Robertson County Hunting Preserve
Rt. 3
Brooksville, KY 41004
Q,P,C,* six months

Shelby County
Whistling Quail
Rt. 1
Bagdad, KY 40003
(502) 747-8786
Q,C,P,* September 1–May 15

Union County
Watson Pheasant Farm
Rt. 5, Box 144
Morganfield, KY 42437
(502) 389-3085
P,Q,C,*** September 1–April 15

LOUISIANA
Season: October 1–April 30
License: In-state, $5.50

Union Parish
Wild Wings Hunting Preserve
Rt. 2, Box 290
Downsville, LA 71234
(318) 982-7777
Q,P,C,M.Huns*** October 1–April 30

MARYLAND
Season: October 1–March 31
License: Special nonresident, $3.50

Kent County
Hopkins Game Farm
Kennedyville, MD 21645
(301) 348-5287
P,Q,C,* October 1–March 31

Queen Anne's County
Native Shore Hunting Preserve
Rt. #3, Box 80
Centreville, MD 21617
(301) 758-0133
P,Q,C,Ducks,Geese,*** October 1–March 31

Pheasantfield Shooting Preserve
Rt. 3, Box 245A
Chestertown, MD 21620
(301) 778-0149
P,Q,C,M,Ducks,*** October 1–March 31

Talbot County
Cook's Hope Hunting Service
307 E. Dover St.
Easton, MD 21601
(301) 822-9267
M,P,C,Q,T,Geese,Ducks,*** October 1–March 31

MICHIGAN

Season: August 15–April 30
License: Special preserve, $8.75

Kent County
Pine Hill Sportsman's Club
8347 10 Mile Rd.
Rockford, MI 49341
(616) 874-8459
P,Q,C,*** July 15–April 30

Lapeer County
Bourbon Barrel Hunt Club
1442 N. Summers
Imlay City, MI 48444
(313) 724-8135
P,C,Q,M,*** August 15–April 30

Hunter's Creek Club
675 E. Sutton Rd.
Metamora, MI 48455
(313) 664-4307
P,C,Q,** August 15–April 30

Osceola County
Rendezvous
17865 21 Mile Rd.
Big Rapids, MI 49307
(616) 796-2390
Q,* August 15–April 30

St. Joseph County
Willow Lake Sportsman's Club
51704 U.S. 131

Three Rivers, MI 49093
(616) 279-124
P,C,Q,** September–April

MINNESOTA
Season: September 1–March 31
License: Special nonresident, $11.75

Nicollet County
Pleasant Acres
R.R. 3, Box 144
New Ulm, MN 56073
(507) 359-4166
P,Q,Ducks,Partridge*** September 1–March 31

Washington County
Wild Wings of Oneka
9491 152nd St. North
Hugo, MN 55038
(612) 439-4287
P,C,Q,M,T,Hungarian partridge** September 1–March 31

MISSISSIPPI
Season: September 1–May 30
License: Special nonresident, $3

Holmes & Carroll County
Wilderness West
1104 McDowell Rd.
Jackson, MS 39204
Q,P,T,Ducks*** September 1–March 31

MISSOURI
Season: September 1–May 31
License: Special preserve; $6/season, $3/3 days

Caldwell County
HiPoint Hunting Club
Route 1
Breckenridge, MO 64625

(816) 644-5708

P,Q,C,*** October 1–April 1

Cass County
Baier's Den Kennels & Shooting Preserve
Peculiar, MO 64078
(816) 758-5234
Q,P,C,*** September 1–June 1

Carroll County
Snow White Enterprises
Rt. 1, Box 40
Carrollton, MO 64633
(816) 542-3037
Q,C,P,* September 1–May 31

Warren County
Tall Oaks Club
Rt. 3, Box 202
Warrenton, MO 63383
(314) 456-3564
P,C,Q,M,Hungarian partridge*** September 1–May 31

NEW JERSEY
Season: September 1–March 15
License: Nonresident one-day small-game, $5.25

Hunterdon County
B & B Pheasantry & Shooting Preserve
Pittstown, NJ 08867
(201) 735-6501
P,C,Q,* September 1–March 15

Burjans Kennel & Game Farm
RD 1, Box 92A
Flemington, NJ 08822
(201) 782-7654
P,Q,C,** September 1–March 15

Salem County
Provident Farm Hunting Preserve

R.R. 3, Box 336
Sharptown, Auburn Rd.
Woodstown, NJ 08098
(609) 769-0116
P,Q,C,M,*** September 1–March 15
M & M Hunting Preserve
Hook & Winston Rds.
Pennsville, NJ 08070
(609) 935-1230
P,C,Q,D September 1–March 15

Cape May and *Cumberland Counties*
Belleplain Farms Shooting Preserve
Box 222, Handsmill Rd.
Belleplain, NJ 08270
P,C,Q,*** September 1–March 15

Gloucester County
Oak Lane Farms
Dutch Mill Rd.
Newfield, NJ 08344
(609) 697-2196
P,M,Q,** September 1–March 15

Sussex County
Big Spring Game Farm
RD 3, Box 591
Haggerty Rd.
Sussex, NJ 07461
(201) 875-3373
September 1–March 15

NEW MEXICO
Lea County
North Lea County Shooting Preserve
Rt. 1
Lovington, NM 88260
(505) 396-4024/396-3441
M,C,Q,P,*** September 1–March 31

NEW YORK

Season: September 1–March 31
License: None required

Allegany County
Valhalla Hunting Preserve
RD 2
Andover, NY 14806
(607) 478-8188/8400
P,Q,C,M,*** September 1–March 31

Delaware County
Catskill Pheasantry
P.O. Box 42
Long Eddy, NY 12760
(914) 887-4487
P,* September 1–March 31

Dutchess County
T-M-T Hunting Preserve
RR 1, Box 297
School House Rd.
Staatsburg, NY 12580
(914) 266-5108
P,Q,C,* September 1–March 31

Orange County
Stonegate Hunting Preserve
Beattie Rd.
Rock Tavern, NY 12575
(914) 427-2115
P,Q,C,*** (September 1–March 31

Orleans County
Forrestel Farm Hunting Preserve
4660 Water Works Rd.
Medina, NY 14103
(716) 798-0222
P,M,Ducks,Geese*** September 1–March 31

Suffolk County
Spring Farm
P.O. Box 301
Sag Harbor, NY 11963
(516) 725-0038
P,M,C,** September 1 March 31

NORTH CAROLINA
Season: October 1–March 31
License: Nonresident preserve, $10

Cleveland County
Lowe's Shooting Preserve
Rt. 1, Box 13
Lawndale, NC 28090
(704) 538-7254
Q,P,*** October 1–March 31

Pender County
Genteel Plantation
Rt. 1, Box 31
Atkinson, NC 28421
(919) 283-5298
Q,* October 1–March 31

Randolph County
Shady Knoll Bird Corp. & Shooting Preserve
Rt. 1, Box 35
Asheboro, NC 27203
(919) 879-3663
Q,P,C,*** November 28–February 28

Richmond County
Derby Hunting Preserve
Rt. 1, Box 469
Jackson Springs, NC 27281
(919) 652-5752
Q,** October 1–March 31

Sampson County
Georgi Hi Plantation
P.O. Box 1068
Roseboro, NC 28382
(919) 525-4524
Q,M,* five months

NORTH DAKOTA
Season: September 1–March 31
License: Resident or nonresident general small game required

Burleigh County
Burnt Creek
#1 Kennel Rd.
Baldwin, ND 58521
(701) 258-6373
P,*** September 1–March 31

Grand Forks County
Dakota Hunting Club & Kennels
Box 1643
Grand Forks, ND 58206
(701) 775-2074
P,C,Q,T,Ducks, Hungarian Partridge*** September 1–March 31

OHIO
Season: September 1–April 30
License: Nonresident preserve, $5.75

Ashland County
Tallmadge Pheasant Farm & Shooting Preserve
16 County Rd. 1950
Jeromesville, OH 44840
(419) 368-3457
P,* October 1–April 15

Clinton County
Cherrybend Pheasant Farm

2326 Cherrybend Rd.
Wilmington, OH 45177
(513) 584-4269
P,C,Q,*** September 1–April 30

Crawford County
Elkhorn Lake Hunt Club
4146 Klopfenstein Rd.
Bucyrus, OH 44820
(419) 562-6131
P,Q,C, Ducks*** September 1–April 30

Hocking County
Hidden Haven Shooting Preserve
9257 Buckeye Rd.
Sugar Grove, OH 43155
P,Q,C, Ducks*** September 1–April 30

Lorain County
Beaver Creek Hunt Club
RD 2, Cooper Foster Rd.
Amherst, OH 44001
(216) 988-88884
P,Q,C,** September 1–April 30

Wayne County
Wooster Duck & Pheasant Hunting Preserve
470 Carter Dr.
Wooster, OH 44691
(216) 262-1671
P,*** October–May

OKLAHOMA
Season: All year
License: 10-day permit, $1

Noble County
Crossed Arrows
Rt. 1, Box 69
Marland, OK 74644

(405) 268-3244
Q,P,***

Okmulgee County
Double W Ranch Kennels & Preserve
Rt. 1, Box 511
Beggs, OK 74421
(918) 827-3188
Q,P,C,***

PENNSYLVANIA
Season: September 1–April 30
License: Nonresident, $3.50/3 days

Blair County
Hillendale Hunting Club
RD 1, Box 168A
Tyrone, PA 16686
(814) 684-5015
P,C,*** September–April

Crawford County
Flying Feather Shooting Preserve
RD 2, Box 343
Guy Mills, PA 16327
P,Q,C,*** September 1–April 30

Fayette County
T.N.T. Shooting Grounds
RD 1, Box 147A
Smock, PA 15480
(412) 677-4620
P,Q,C,* September 1–March 31

Lackawanna County
Marsh Brook Game Preserve
RD 2, Box 109
Factoryville, PA 18419
(717) 222-4469
P,C,M,Q,*** September 1–April 30

Lancaster County
Wilderness Farm
RD 1, Box 337M
Strasburg, PA 17579
(717) 687-8364
P,C,Q,* September–April

Northumberland County
Martz's Game Farm-Gap View Hunting Preserve
RD 1, Box 85
Dalmatia, PA 17017
(717) 758-3307
P,Q,*** September–March

Westmoreland County
Angus Conservation & Hunting Farm
RD 1, Box 260
Latrobe, PA 15650
P,C,Q,*** September–March

RHODE ISLAND
Season: September 1–April 15
License: Preserve, $3.50

Providence County
Addieville East Farm
Box 157
Mapleville, RI 02839
(401) 568-3185
P,C,Q,* September 1–April 15

SOUTH CAROLINA
Season: October 1–March 31
License: Out-of-state, $22

Abbeville County
Rolling Hills Hunting Preserve
Rt. 1
Calhoun Falls, SC 29628

(803) 391-2901
Q October 1–March 31

Aiken County
Oak Ridge Hunting Preserve
Rt. 2, Box 654
Aiken, SC 29801
(803) 648-3489
Q,* October 1–April 1

Laurens County
Single Tree Shooting Preserve
Rt. 1, Box 564
Clinton, SC 29325
(803) 833-5477
Q,P,* October 1–March 31

Orangeburg County
Santee Cooper Shooting Preserve
P.O. Box 187
Elloree, SC 29047
(803) 854-2495 & 897-2731
Q,P,C,* October 15–March 31

SOUTH DAKOTA
Season: September 1–March 31
License: Nonresident general hunting, $2

Kingsburg County
Wells Shooting Preserve
Rt. 1, Box 44
Oldham, SD 57051
(605) 854-3284
P,Q,*** September 1–April 30

TENNESSEE
Cumberland County
Renegade Hunting Range
P.O. Box 741
Crossville, TN 38555

(615) 484-9112
T, Big Game,* All year

TEXAS

Season: October 1–April 1
License: No special preserve license. Out-of-state
      nonresident small game, $37.50

Llano County
Central Texas Hunting Co.
Box 154
Llano, TX 78643
(915) 247-4797
Q,* three months; Deer, six weeks

Montague County
Running High Hunting Club
P.O. Box 1831
Bowie, TX 76230
(817) 934-6300, All year

Shelby County
Hawkeye Hunting Club
P.O. Box 27
Center, TX 75935
(409) 598-2424
P,C,Q, Ducks** six months

UTAH

Box Elder County
Pheasant Valley
P.O. Box 86
Howell, UT 84316
(801) 471-2245
P,M,Q,C,*** September 1–March 31

Emery County
Hatt's Ranch
Box 275
Green River, UT 84525

(801) 564-3238
Q,C,P,*** September 1–March 31

Washington County
Rancho Vue Desert
Bud & Mike Branham
LB 97-3
Hurricane, UT 84737
(801) 639-2340
P,C,* six months

VERMONT
Season: September 1–March 31
License: None required

Windham County
Hermitage Inn Hunting Preserve
Box 457, Coldbrook Rd.
Wilmington, VT 05363
(802) 464-3511
P,C,Q, Woodcock, Grouse,*** September 1–March 31

Rutland County
Tinmouth Hunting Preserve
RFD Tinmouth Box 556
Wallingford, VT 05773
(802) 446-2337
P,Q,C,* September 1–March 31

VIRGINIA
Season: October 1–March 31
License: Nonresident preserve, $7.50

Prince William County
Merrimac Farm Hunting Preserve
14710 Deepwood Ln.
Nokesville, VA 22123
(703) 594-2276
P,Q,C,*** October 1–March 31

Please add my family to the

Burger Brothers

mailing list. We are looking forward to receiving seasonal family sporting tips and advance notice of seminar and sales events.

PLEASE PRINT:

Name _____

Address _____

City _____

State _____ Zip _____

Age _____ Phone _____

Interested in information on:

☐ Fishing   ☐ Hunting   ☐ Camping

☐ Other _____

Jarvis City — PA
Benton Pa
→ 800-836-6545

PRIMLAND
Claudville VA (703) 251-8012

WASHINGTON

Yakima County
Triple B. Hunting & Cons. Club
Rt. 1, Box 1855
Selah, WA 98942
(509) 697-7675
Q,P,C, Ducks,*** August 15–March 31

WISCONSIN

Season: All year, but call each preserve for its season
License: None required

Columbia County
Martin Fish & Game Farm
Rt. 3, Hwy. 127
Portage, WI 53901
(608) 742-7205
P,Q,C,T, Huns, Ducks,*** 12 months

Dodge County
Pleasant View Farm
184 Garfield Rd.
Rt. 1, Box 200
Neosho, WI 53059
(414) 625-3854
P,** 12 months

Douglas County
Bydand Kennels & Shooting Grounds
Maple, WI 54854
(715) 363-2347
P,Q,* 12 months

Fond du Lac County
Pheasant City
Rt. 1
Markesan, WI 53946
(414) 324-5813
P,Q,C,*** September–April

Wild Wings Hunting & Fishing Preserve
870 Hwy. W. Rt. 4
Campbellsport, WI 53010
(414) 533-8738
P,T,C,Q, Ducks*** September 1–April 1

Kenosha County
Halter Wildlife
9626 113th St.
Kenosha, WI 53142
(414) 697-0070
P,C,T,Q,** 12 months

Manitowoc County
Thunderbird Game Farm
Leonard P. Leberg
Rt. 4, Box 193, Thunderbird Rd.
Chilton, WI 53014
(414) 853-3030
P,T,** September 15–March 30

Sheboygan County
Blue Wing Hunt Club
Rt. 1, Box 117
Elkhart Lake, WI 53020
(414) 894-3318
P,** September 1–April 1

Hawe Hunting Preserve
Rt. 1, Box 115A
Waldo, WI 53093
(414) 528-8388
P,C,Q,M,T,*** September 15–April 1

Shawano County
S & H Game Farm
RR 1, Box 221
Shiocton, WI 54170
(715) 758-8134
P,** October 1–March 31

Vilas County, WI & Iron County, MI
Smoky Lake Reserve
1 Lake St., P.O. Box 100
Phelps, WI 54554
(715) 545-2333
*P,C,Q,T, Ducks**

Winnebago County
Pheasant Retreat Game Farm
Rt. 2, 2190 Prellwitz Rd.
Ripon, WI 54971
(414) 748-9427
P,*** October 1–April 1

WYOMING

Johnson County
The Covey
P.O. Box 8
Buffalo, WY 82834
(307) 684-2271
P,Q,C, August 1–February 28

Tailfeathers Hunting Club
Box 783
Riverton, WY 82501
(307) 856-1618
P,Q,C,** August–February

CANADA
Season: All year, but call each club for its season
License: None required

Manitoba-Springfield
Springfield Game Farm
GR. 4, Box 6, Rt. 1
Anola, Manitoba, Canada ROE-OAO
(204) 866-2624
P,Q,C,T,* September 1–April 30

Province of Ontario
The Wild Wings Club
RR 4
Fenwick, Ontario
Canada LOS-1CO
(416) 892-5930
P,C,Q,** All year

Essex County
Willowood Game Farm
Rt. 2, Box 123
Amherstburg, Ontario
Canada N9V-2Y8
(519) 736-5207
P,C,*** All year

Northbrook, Ontario
Lennox & Addington
RR 1, Flinton, Ontario
Canada KOH-1PO
(613) 336-8552
P,*

Ontario
Pine Ridge Hunting Preserve
RR 5
Sunderland, Ontario, Canada LOC-1HO
(416) 985-8824
P,C,Q, All year

Prince Edward
Waupoos Island Pheasant Farm
RR 4
Picton, Ontario, Canada KOK-2TO
(613) 476-3910
P,T, from September 1

Index

173